WALKS FOR ALL AGES
ESSEX

WALKS *FOR*
ALL AGES

ESSEX

CLIVE BROWN

BRADWELL
BOOKS

Published by Bradwell Books
9 Orgreave Close Sheffield S13 9NP
Email: books@bradwellbooks.co.uk

1st Edition

ISBN: 9781910551127

Print: Gomer Press, Llandysul, Ceredigion SA44 4JL

Design by: Andrew Caffrey. **Typesetting and mapping by:** Mark Titterton

Photograph Credits: Photographs © Clive Brown, Visit Essex (p.2, p.7, p.16-17, p. 22-3, p.52-3). Other images are credited separately.

Maps: Contain Ordnance Survey data
© Crown copyright and database right 2016

Ordnance Survey licence number 100039353

The information in this book has been produced in good faith and is intended as a general guide. Although the maps in this book are based on original Ordnance Survey mapping, walkers are always advised to use a detailed OS map. Look in 'The Basics' section for recommendations for the most suitable map for each of the walks.

Bradwell Books and the authors have made all reasonable efforts to ensure that the details are correct at the time of publication. Bradwell Books and the authors cannot accept responsibility for any changes that have taken place subsequent to the book being published.

It is the responsibility of individuals undertaking any of the walks listed in this book to exercise due care and consideration for their own health and wellbeing and that of others in their party. The walks in this book are not especially strenuous, but individuals taking part should ensure they are fit and well before setting off.

A good pair of walking books is essential for these walks. It is advisable to take good-quality waterproofs, and if undertaking the walks during the winter, take plenty of warm clothing as well. Because the walks will take some time, it would be a good idea to take along some food and drink.

Enjoy walking. Enjoy Essex with Bradwell Books!

CONTENTS

INTRODUCTION

ON FIRST IMPRESSION THE COUNTY OF ESSEX SEEMS TO DIVIDE NEATLY INTO TWO HALVES: THE CROWDED SUBURBAN SOUTH WITH ITS BUSY INDUSTRIAL TOWNS ALONG THE THAMES ESTUARY AND NEAT RANKS OF MODERN HOUSING STRETCHING OUT OF SIGHT; AND THE EMPTY AND AGRICULTURAL RURAL NORTH, WITH ITS ENDLESS LITTLE VILLAGES REACHED BY NARROW LANES, THE HALF-TIMBERED HOUSES SPRAWLED AROUND A VILLAGE GREEN. IN REALITY THERE ARE SOME BEAUTIFUL PARTS OF THE COUNTY IN THE SOUTH. TO THE EAST THE LAND IS VERY FLAT, TAILING OFF IN ENDLESS MUD FLATS AND SALT MARSH; A PARADISE FOR BIRDWATCHERS AND NATURE LOVERS.

This book scratches the surface of the walking routes available in the county. Epping Forest features in only one walk yet there are plenty more paths and tracks to discover. Other areas worth exploring are Thorndon Country Park near Brentwood, Danbury Common and village near Chelmsford and Dedham Vale along the River Stour on the border with Suffolk.

The Roman fort of Caesaromagus existed at the confluence of the rivers Can and Chelmer during the Roman Era. The settlement's name became Ceolmaer's Ford in Saxon times and Celmeresfort in the Domesday Book. By the end of the 12th century, after the building of a bridge and the granting of the Royal Charter giving permission to hold a market, the town had become Chelmsford. The church of St Mary's became a cathedral, the second smallest in England. Chelmsford had to wait until the Queen's Diamond Jubilee celebrations of 2012 before it was granted city status.

Colchester's proud boast is that it is the oldest town in England. The settlement had been founded towards the end of the Iron Age, not long before the arrival of the Romans, who invaded Britain in AD 43. After the Legions moved on and the town became Camulodunum; a colonia or centre for retired soldiers, bringing Roman culture to the area. After the death of the Emperor Claudius in AD 54, he was immediately deified and a magnificent temple built in the town to worship him; its centrepiece was a life-size bronze figure.

The complacency of the Roman settlers was shattered in 61AD; King Prasutagus of the Iceni died and left his widow and their two daughters in the care of the Roman Empire. Historically Rome had little regard for the rights of women; the daughters were raped and Queen Boudicca badly beaten up. Boudicca and the Iceni led a popular revolt against

Rome destroying Colchester and burning the survivors alive in Claudius's Temple. The bronze statue was smashed to pieces; amazingly the severed head was found in 1907 by a boy swimming in the River Alde in Suffolk and it can still be seen in the British Museum. Boudicca and her army went on to destroy London and St Albans before being massacred by a Roman Army from the north-west.

Essex is a stronghold of the art of pargeting, relief or 3D decorations in the plasterwork between the studs (wooden struts) of half-timbered, wooden frame houses. The artwork sometimes covers the whole of the first floor walls of a building. Simple designs were made using just a shaped piece of wood, while more complex shapes were made with fingers and templates and occasionally with pre-shaped sections.

Every village in the county seems to have its own derelict World War II airfield. At certain times of day towards the end of the war, the skies above Essex must have been black with aircraft. The county is also well provided with Local Nature Reserves (LNR) and Sites of Special Scientific Interest (SSSI). Essex Wildlife Trust look after nine visitor centres, two nature parks and 87 local nature reserves.

visitessex.com

CABBAGE WOOD

Most of Debden Water to the right on the first half of the walk is a Site of Special Scientific Interest. Debden Water flows east to join the River Cam, while not far away at Debden Green is the source of the River Chelmer flowing in the opposite direction.

Before the advent of the M11 motorway the road through Newport was the A11, carrying considerably more traffic as it was then the main route from London to Norwich. A toll was once charged for crossing the bridge over the river at the northern end of the village; a noticeboard on the Toll House Bed and Breakfast gives a list of the charges which were levied. Saxon names for towns with markets often had the suffix port.

Debden Hall was purchased by Richard Chiswell in the early 18th century. His ancestor Richard had the hall rebuilt by the architect Henry Holland in 1795. At the turn of the 19th century it was in the possession of the financier, industrialist and politician the 1st Baron Strathcona and Mount Royal. On his death his daughter the 2nd Baroness inherited, but the hall was considered too expensive to run and it descended into decay. It was demolished in 1936.

Newport High Street is full of interesting buildings; Monk's Barn is probably the most remarkable. It is a typical Wealden House, called this because the design is normally found only in the Weald of Kent and sometimes south-east England. The house is timber framed with four bays, the two middle ones making a hall open to the roof with a central fireplace/ hearth. Early examples had thatched roofs and wattle-and-daub walls; later houses became more sophisticated with overhanging jetties on the first floor, tiled roofs and brick infilling to the walls. Monk's Barn has a brick infill in a herringbone pattern.

The railway line through Newport Station is the West Anglia Main Line from Liverpool Street in London to Cambridge and King's Lynn. Permission for the line was given by Parliament to the Northern and Eastern company in 1836 but by 1843 it had only managed to reach Bishop's Stortford. The Eastern Counties Railway took over the operations and soon got things moving, and the station and the line to Cambridge and Norwich was opened in 1845. The line had originally used a gauge of 5 feet (1,524mm), but sanity soon prevailed and the lines and rolling stock changed to the standard gauge of 4 feet 8½ inches (1,435mm).

THE BASICS

Distance: 6 miles / 9.6km

Gradient: Several easy slopes

Severity: Easy

Approx. time to walk: 3 hours

Stiles: Several stiles and gates

Maps: OS Landranger 154 (Cambridge and Newmarket) and 167 (Chelmsford); Explorer 195 (Braintree and Saffron Walden)

Path description: Hard tracks, grassy fields, field edges and wider hardcore farm roads

Start point: The corner of High Street and Station Road, Newport, (GR TL 521337)

Parking: Sensible roadside parking in the village; bus service (check details) (CB11 3PL)

Dog friendly: Not brilliant for dogs; several stiles and a busy road to cross

Public toilets: None

Nearest food: The Coach and Horses, Cambridge Road (CB11 3TR)

CABBAGE WOOD WALK

1. Take the High Street and Belmont Hill north to Water Lane on the right, turn right and go under the railway arch. Keep straight on up the wide concrete access road, over the stream and passing right of the sewage works. Continue with the field to the right and the high ground to the left, to the marker post at the corner of the trees. Bear slight right, with the trees to the left to the far corner.

2. Keep direction, through the trees, past the footbridge with the stream Debden Water still to the right. Carry on left of the telegraph pole with the hedge still right, past a marker post close to some open ground. Follow the path left over a stile and walk up to the stile at the end by the black wooden garage. Cross and turn right, down the driveway to the road.

3. Turn sharp left up the farm driveway to the marker post on the right and turn right, up the track parallel to the telegraph poles. At the corner of Howe Wood, bear right along the bridleway/farm track to the road.

4. Keep direction over the road and through the trees, continue up the hill over the concrete area (watch out for the concealed cattle grid). Follow the hardcore road bearing right, through the gap in the trees and over the bridge straddling the end of the lake.

5. Carry on uphill into Cabbage Wood and follow the track through to the other side. Exit through the massive iron kissing gate and take the wide gritty farm road, past the buildings at Waldegraves, to the road at a corner.

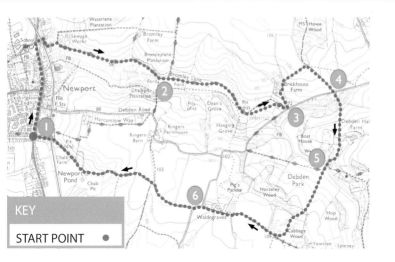

KEY

START POINT ●

6. Keep straight on, slightly left and take the farm road to the right/straight on. The path wanders past some trees, the other side of which is a disused chalk quarry, and leads eventually down to the station. Cross the footbridge and follow Station Road ahead to the High Street.

CASTLE HEDINGHAM

HEDINGHAM CASTLE IS THE ANCESTRAL SEAT OF THE DE VERE FAMILY, EARLS OF OXFORD; GIVEN BY WILLIAM I TO AUBREY DE VERE IN 1086. THE CASTLE WAS COMPLETED BY THE MIDDLE OF THE TWELFTH CENTURY. THE KEEP IS THE ONLY REMAINING PART OF THE ORIGINAL STRUCTURE; OTHER PARTS HAVE BEEN DISMANTLED AND REBUILT MORE THAN ONCE OVER THE CENTURIES.

Several members of the de Vere family have left their mark on English history. It was the third Aubrey de Vere who became the first Earl in 1141. The third Earl was a signatory of Magna Carta. Two hundred years later the 11th Earl was fighting at the Battle of Agincourt but died two years after, aged only 31. His son John de Vere, the 12th Earl, took the Lancastrian side in the Wars of the Roses and both he and his elder son Aubrey were beheaded in 1462. John de Vere's second son, also John, became the 13th Earl and had a pivotal role  in English history. Henry Tudor, although the de facto Lancastrian leader, had little military experience and relied on the advice of the Earl during the Battle of Bosworth Field.

A hundred years later the family seems to have changed a little. The Earls became patrons of the arts; Edward, the 17th Earl, had something of a reputation as a playwright and poet; his name is one of those put forward as the 'real' author of the works of Shakespeare. Another Aubrey, born in 1627, the 20th and last of the Earls, fought on the Royalist side in the Civil War. He died with no male heir and there were no other claimants to be Earl of Oxford. The title is, however, classed as dormant rather than extinct, and the present owner, Thomas Lindsay, can trace his ancestry to the de Veres through both his father and mother.

Two blue plaques on houses in Castle Hedingham commemorate famous residents. Mark Catesby was born in the village in 1682. Catesby was financially comfortable after the death of his father and in 1714 left on a long visit to his sister in Virginia, returning in 1719 via the West Indies. An avid student of natural history since childhood, Catesby brought back a considerable collection of specimens and information. He undertook a further expedition from 1722 to 1726 and spent the rest of his life producing illustrations of his collection and the book Natural History of Carolina, Florida and the Bahama Islands.

The other plaque remembers Eric Ravilious, born in London in 1903. He became an artist and wood engraver and married fellow artist Tirzah Garwood, coming to live in Bank House in Castle Hedingham in 1934. Ravilious worked mainly in watercolours but also branched out into woodcuts, book illustration and ceramic design. At the start of the Second World War Ravilious became a war artist, producing some iconic work illustrating aspects of naval warfare during the first part of the war. The story has a tragic ending, however; in 1942 he went on a trip to an RAF station in Iceland, where he joined a search party looking for a missing aereoplane, but his own aircraft was also lost.

The village was the birthplace of Sir Fowell Buxton (1786–1845) who was an anti-slavery campaigner, taking over leadership of the movement after the retirement of William Wilberforce. In 1824, he was the founding chairman of the organisation which became the Royal Society for the Prevention of Cruelty to Animals (RSPCA). He also helped his sister-in-law Elizabeth Fry with prison reform. Sir Fowell Buxton was the grandfather of Edward North Buxton; see the information under Hatfield Forest (Walk no 11).

THE BASICS

Distance: 3¾ miles / 6km

Gradient: Several easy slopes

Severity: Easy

Approx. time to walk: 1¾ to 2 hours

Stiles: Several stiles and gates

Maps: OS Landranger 155 (Bury St Edmunds); Explorer 195 (Braintree and Saffron Walden)

Path description: Hard paths, grassy fields, field edges and wider hardcore farm roads. A short section crosses a field which may be muddy in the wet

Start point: Falcon Square, Castle Hedingham (GR TL 784355)

Parking: Sensible roadside parking in the village; bus service (check details) (CO9 3BY)

Dog friendly: Several stiles not adapted for dogs

Public toilets: None

Nearest food: The Bell Inn, the Wheatsheaf Inn, the Old Moot House Restaurant and Buckley's Tea Rooms

CASTLE HEDINGHAM WALK

1. Take Sudbury Road to the east, away from the village, on the roadside path to the signpost on the left at the '40' sign. Turn left up this enclosed path through trees and along a right-hand field edge and the corner of the field which may be under cultivation although a path should be well marked within any crop, to the road, Rosemary Lane.

2. Turn left along this road and follow as it curves left and right to a marker post on the left as the road turns to the right again. Bear left over the metal-railed footbridge and through the wide metal gate to the fence corner on the left, bear further left over the stile in the far corner. Keep ahead on left-hand field edges with the hedge and trees to the left through the corner at the end. Keep direction to the end, with the hedge still left down to the road.

3. Go left down to the T-junction, cross and take the roadside path to the right; down and over the bridge to the footpath signpost on the left at the bus stop. Turn left along the path with the River Colne to the left to the marker post at the wide metal gate. Follow the path through the undergrowth with the trees and the hedge to the right, bearing right through the kissing gate. Continue through the trees with the fence to the left, to the road.

4. Turn left, over the bridge to the signpost and take the path right, with the Colne now to the right. Carry on through the edge of the trees, bearing right at the end to a junction of tracks near a large house. Take the wide driveway left with the fence and the trees to the right, to the road.

5. Cross and pass the signpost, and walk up the field edge with the dyke to the right, passing left of a power line pole. Keep on this track, left and right at the corners and left and right where the reservoir is hidden in the trees. The track continues up the slight slope with the fence and the hedge to the right, to a marker post on the right.

6. Turn left, past the tree and keep straight on across the open field which should have a path well marked within any crop, to the hedge ahead. Turn right, along the field edge and take the path bearing left, through the hedge gap, down a slope through trees, past the barrier, down the steps and carefully cross the road to the roadside path. Turn left back into the village and your starting point.

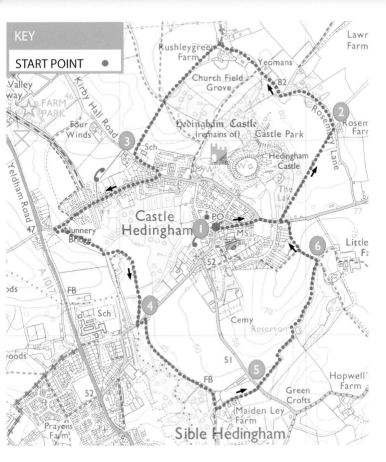

KEY

START POINT ●

COGGESHALL

Coggeshall is a town full of interesting architecture containing several significant buildings; over 300 of these are listed and many more houses considered fairly ordinary here would be given special status in any other town.

Grange Barn was built by the Abbey in the 13th century, it is one of the oldest timber-framed buildings in the world. Braintree District Council bought the barn in 1982 and completed restoration in 1985. The council gave the barn to the National Trust who opened the building to the public. It now contains a display of farm wagons and carts.

The church of St Peter ad Vincula (St Peter in chains) is one of the largest churches in Essex and regarded as a 'wool church', built during the 15th century by benefactors who became rich in the wool trade. Nearby St Nicholas' Chapel was the gatehouse chapel for the Abbey; it had been built in about 1220 using bricks made by the monks themselves. It is thought to be the oldest brick building built in this country since the departure of the Romans.

The Abbey was founded in 1140 by Queen Matilda. It thrived on farming its land and manufacturing and trading in wool products. The monks also had their own mill and made bricks. The Romans had made bricks in England but the trade had died out. During the Dark Ages bricks for building were taken from derelict Roman buildings; the Abbey at Coggeshall was one of the first places to begin making bricks again. The dissolution of the Abbey came in 1538. The Abbey church itself was dismantled and the stone and other fabric sold for building materials. Some of the other buildings still survive behind the mill complex, seen on the right approaching point 5.

The mill itself is thought to be mainly 17th century; it housed various processes connected to the textile trade. After the decline of this business it worked until 1960 grinding corn and other grains. The mill is still in working order but not open to the public.

The clock tower on Market Hill has quite a convoluted history. The original clock and a bell were installed in a building used as a market hall in the centre of the thoroughfare. This hall fell into disrepair and was demolished in 1795. Cranes House was being used as a schoolroom and the clock and bell were moved there into a specially built turret. As the Golden Jubilee of Queen Victoria approached in 1887 the town decided to build a commemorative clock tower in the clock's original position, but not enough money could be raised. The townspeople arrived at the obvious solution of buying a new clock and installing it and the bell in a higher, more impressive tower.

One of the town's most interesting characters was the blacksmith Dick Nunn. Dick had been apprenticed to his father and took over the business at 18 when his father died. He had strongly held views and often just went ahead with things to get them done. The footbridge over the River Blackwater on the public footpath between points 3 and 4 collapsed in 1875 and no one would do anything about it. This went on for 17 years until Dick could wait no longer; he built the flimsy-looking but sturdy metal bridge in his workshop. He balanced the new bridge on two trolleys and wheeled it into position. This beautiful piece of workmanship is still known as Nunn's Bridge.

THE BASICS

Distance: 3¾ miles / 6km

Gradient: A couple of very easy slopes

Severity: Easy

Approx. time to walk: 1¾ hours

Stiles: None, gates only

Maps: OS Landranger 168 (Colchester); Explorer 195 (Braintree and Saffron Walden)

Path description: Grassy fields, field edges and wider hardcore farm roads

Start point: From the car park behind the council offices in Stoneham Street, Coggeshall (GR TL 849227)

Parking: Use the car park behind the council offices in Stoneham Street (pay and display) (CO6 1UH)

Dog friendly: Gates only, but would need to be on a lead in the town streets

Public toilets: Close to the car park

Nearest food: Loads of opportunities in town

COGGESHALL WALK

1. Go back towards the car park entrance past the tiny park to the path on the left. Turn left between the low wall and the hedge curving left past the council offices and cross the bridge over the stream to the crossroads of paths. Bear right between fields and keep ahead through the far left corner. Continue between fields, to a tarmac driveway.

2. Cross and keep straight on, conifers to your right and then a wall to the left. Go through a wooden kissing gate and down a left-hand field edge with the house to the left, through the next kissing gate and up to the road. Cross this busy road carefully and turn right to the signpost.

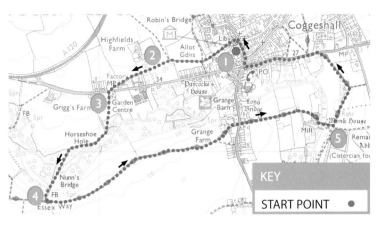

KEY

START POINT •

3. Turn left through the potholed parking area and turn left, then right, between fences. Go down the wooden steps at the end. Turn left, then right, between trees with the River Blackwater to the left. The path meanders along to elegant Nunn's Bridge footbridge. Cross and keep straight on, over the footbridge at the end and bear left up the field edge with the hedge to the left, to the farm road at the top.

4. Take the road left, all the way to the road passing left of Grange Farm. Cross this busy road carefully and carry on up the potholed road ahead passing right of St Nicholas' Chapel. Keep straight on right, bearing right of the house, and turn left over streams to the crossroads of tracks.

5. Turn left, with the willows to the left, go over the concrete driveway and keep direction through the kissing gate, all the way to the road. Turn left along the roadside path back to the town centre and right, up to the clock tower; the passageway to the left leads left and right, back to the car park.

visitessex.com

COPPERAS BAY

The walk goes through the centre of Stour Wood, a Site of Special Scientific Interest (SSSI). It continues into Copperas Wood, which was badly damaged during the 1987 hurricane; parts of the wood have been left as they were to measure the effect of such damage on wildlife. The mudflats on the shoreline of Copperas Bay are one of the most important wintering sites for waders.

The iconic 'Julie's House', also known as 'A House for Essex', can be seen from various parts of the walk. The house was completed in 2015 and is actually a holiday home which can be rented by the general public. It was created by the ceramics artist Grayson Perry, also well known for his cross dressing. Julie's House celebrates the fictional story of Essex-born Julie May Cope.

At first sight the house achieves its design aim, appearing on the skyline as a Christian Orthodox chapel. The flamboyant and exotic aspect of this tile-clad edifice, topped by a pregnant naked woman and a giant vase, are not apparent until seen from closer up. A path leads from the route of the walk between points 5 and 6 up to the house.

Wrabness is surrounded by nature reserves; Oakfield Wood is a natural burial site which when full will become a Local Nature Reserve. The Essex Way leads further west to Wrabness Nature Reserve which was originally an Admiralty Mine Supply Depot. These depots were situated away from homes and vulnerable military areas to facilitate the dangerous process of supplying armaments to Royal Navy ships. The depot closed in

1963, and during the succeeding years no decision was taken on its further use although several planning applications were turned down, including two attempts to build a prison here. The site is now looked after by the Essex Wildlife Trust.

The railway line runs between Manningtree and Harwich, the passenger service marketed as the Mayflower Line. It also carries a considerable amount of freight, particularly containers, to and from the port of Harwich and Parkeston Quay.

All Saints Church was built in the years succeeding the Norman Invasion. The church originally had a spire which collapsed in the 17th century; the wooden bell cage was built as a temporary measure.

The impressive building with the tall spire seen across the estuary is the Royal Hospital School. The school was founded in 1712 and originally shared premises with the Greenwich Hospital, in what is now the National Maritime Museum. The school moved to its present location in 1933.

THE BASICS

Distance: 4½ miles / 7.25km

Gradient: Several easy slopes

Severity: Easy

Approx. time to walk: 2¼ hours

Stiles: None, gates only

Maps: OS Landranger 169 (Ipswich and the Naze); Explorer 184 (Colchester)

Path description: Woodland tracks, quiet roads, hard paths, field edges and wider hardcore farm roads

Start point: The car park at Oakfield Wood, Church Road, Wrabness (GR TM 171317); or the station car park in Wrabness village (GR TM 181315)

Parking: The car park at Oakfield Wood, (CO11 2TQ); or the station car park (CO11 2TL, pay and display). It may also be possible to park on the roadside near the church and start from the instructions there, though maybe not on Sunday mornings!

Dog friendly: Good for dogs

Public toilets: None

Nearest food: Wrabness Community Shop and Café, next to the station

COPPERAS BAY WALK

1. Go back to the road and turn left upslope to the corner; follow this not very busy road to the right, past the church, bearing right, across the bridge over the railway and turn left at the T-junction. Turn left along the roadside path to the station.

2. Keep straight on right of the shop along Black Boy Lane and turn left over the railway bridge. Turn immediate right, on the path parallel to the railway and turn right, back across the narrow bridge to the marker post. Bear left through the kissing gate at the trees. Follow the path and bear right on the wider track through the green barrier, marked RSPB car park. Keep ahead through Stour Wood to the two low signposts pointing in opposite directions.

3. Take the track left marked to the hides, keep on the path nearly to the railway line and carry on to the right, out of the trees and upslope on a narrow path between the railway and an open field. Turn left, back across the railway again.

4. Go through the left-hand wide gate, bear left past a marker post and keep straight on at the junction. Follow the path left with the shoreline to the right.

5. Continue on this path for a mile and a half (2km), with Copperas Bay on the right, to the footpath signpost at the corner of the caravan site.

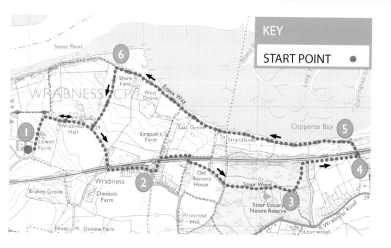

6. Turn left, up this wide access lane, past the gate at the top and on to the road passed near the beginning of the walk. Retrace your steps back to your starting point.

EAST MERSEA FLATS

THE ISLAND 12 MILES FROM COLCHESTER IS 5 MILES (8KM) LONG, 2 MILES (3.2KM) WIDE AND ABOUT 8 SQUARE MILES (25 SQ. KM) IN AREA. IT IS DIVIDED VERY NEATLY INTO TWO; THE LARGER MORE COMMERCIALISED WEST MERSEA WITH ITS HOLIDAY HOMES, GUEST HOUSES, SHOPS AND RESTAURANTS AND THE SMALLER, QUIETER EAST MERSEA, WITH ITS CARAVAN AND CAMP SITES, CUDMORE GROVE COUNTRY PARK AND EXTENSIVE MUD FLATS TEEMING WITH WILDLIFE.

The mud flats play host to a vast range of waders and water birds, resident or migrant, summer and winter. Brent Geese always arrive in large numbers each winter.

The low cliffs at the western end of Cudmore are being eroded year on year. As they disappear into the sea the fossilised bones of animals appear, having been hidden for up to half a million years. Several skeletons of animals considered more at home in the African continent have been found.

The pillbox near the car park is one of a line along the south-east coast of the island, part of the extensive fortifications constructed during the early part of the Second World War when the island was considered to be an invasion risk. There were also searchlight systems, several observation posts and a battery of ex-naval large-calibre guns. Also on this shoreline are the earth ramparts of a fort built to protect the estuary in Tudor/Stuart times.

The Strood, the causeway linking the island with the mainland and carrying the B1025 road, is subject to frequent flooding at high tide and must not be crossed during these events. The oak piles used in its construction have been dated to the late 7th century by dendrochronologists.

The Romans in nearby Colchester (Camulodunum) used Mersea Island as a holiday destination. At least one high-ranking Roman official chose the island as his final resting place. A mound just off the road to East Mersea was excavated in 1912; the archaeologists found a lead-lined casket in which there was an urn containing cremated human remains.

THE BASICS

Distance: 3¼ miles / 5.25km

Gradient: Flat

Severity: Easy

Approx. time to walk: 1½ hours

Stiles: None, gates only

Maps: OS Landranger 168 (Colchester); Explorer 184 (Colchester)

Path description: Mainly grass-topped embankments, grassy fields, hard paths, field edges and one section of not very busy road

Start point: Cudmore Grove Country Park, Bromans Lane, East Mersea (GR TM 065146)

Parking: Cudmore Grove Country Park car park (pay and display). Limited bus service (check details) (CO5 8UE)

Dog friendly: Good for dogs

Public toilets: At the country park

Nearest food: Dog and Pheasant and Mehalah's on East Road; The Company Shed on Coast Road, West Mersea

EAST MERSEA FLATS WALK

1. Walk out of the car park along the wide track mown into the grass, past the concrete pillbox to the path at the coastline and turn left past the East Mersea Flats signpost. Carry on along this rough tarmac path on the top of the embankment.

2. Follow the path left on a less substantial surface, past a large wooden building. Go through a metal kissing gate to the marker post and turn left down the uneven steps.

3. Go through the kissing gate at the dyke and bear right (there is normally a track in the grass) to a marker post at the boundary ahead. Turn left to the next marker post, go across the footbridge and turn left along the path through the trees. Continue up and down the steps and keep ahead on the wider driveway between trees to the T-junction of tracks.

4. Turn right and follow the road left; as the houses on the left end, turn left through the gate/gap, past the almost hidden signpost and along the field edge with the hedge to the left. Carry on between fields to the marker post at the hedge ahead.

5. Take the field edge right, to the marker post in the corner and turn left along the path between hedges and along the gravel drive to the road. Turn right and follow the road left, up to Broman's Lane. Turn left along this access road to the country park car park.

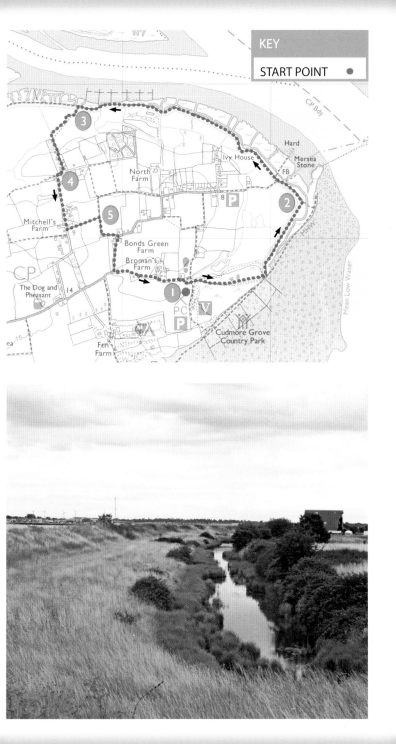

EPPING FOREST

Epping Forest was taken over by the City of London after Parliament passed the Epping Forest Act in 1878. Queen Victoria visited Chingford in 1882 and dedicated 'this beautiful forest to the use and enjoyment of my people for all time'.

The forest is a magical place to visit; there are very few conifers and even fewer rhododendrons. Most of the trees were originally pollarded; the branches were cut off at head height and allowed to grow again. This has not been carried out for a long time and the trees now have substantial branches growing out from the original cuts. As a result the trees now look as though they are about to come alive and wave their branches about like a Disney cartoon fairy tale.

Epping was known as Waltham Forest until the 17th century; it had been developed by the Norman Kings as a Royal Forest. This meant that although commoners could graze livestock and gather food and fuel, only the king could use it for hunting. This right to graze and lop trees for fuel started to disappear during the early years of the 19th century. Landowners started to enclose land and use it for agriculture; speculators also began to develop land to house London's exploding population. The forest began to disappear at an alarming rate but in 1871 the City of London started to prosecute landowners for illegal enclosure. This culminated in the Epping Forest Act, through which the City bought 5,500 acres for £250,000, terminating its status as a Royal forest and the crown's right to hunt within it.

Commoners (people living within the forest) cannot now cut branches from trees for firewood, but still have the right to collect 'one faggot of dead or driftwood per day'. They may also graze their cattle, although this is less frequent today due partly to the danger of busy road traffic.

Epping now consists of 6,118 acres of forest and heath in a narrow swathe of land 12 miles (19km) south of the town of Epping. It sits on a ridge between the rivers Roding and Lee, measuring only 2½ miles (4 km) at its maximum width. The forest has been covered by trees since at least the late Stone Age and possibly longer. The Iron Age Hill Forts at Ambresbury Bank and Loughton Camp probably date back to about 500 BC.

Queen Elizabeth's Hunting Lodge close to Chingford was built by King Henry VIII in 1543 as a grandstand to enable him to watch hunting in progress when he was no longer able to follow on horseback. It was also used as a platform to fire arrows and crossbows bolts at passing deer. The open sides were later filled in and it was then used first as a lodging for VIP huntsmen, and then as a gamekeeper's residence.

The highwayman Dick Turpin is alleged to have had a hiding place within the forest, as well as using its deserted and secluded byways to pursue his trade. The heavy tree cover, easy road access and proximity to London have made the forest a popular place to hide murder victims in fiction as well as fact. Authors Charles Dickens and Dorothy L. Sayers and the TV programmes EastEnders and New Tricks have all used the forest as the setting for dark deeds.

In the past the land behind the King's Oak pub at High Beach was used for motorcycle speedway; it was the first venue for the sport on 19 February 1928. Large numbers of bikers meet on this day each year in High Beach to commemorate the event. The track closed when a swimming pool was built on the site after the war. The village is still a place where large groups of motorcyclists gather to sit and talk about their exploits, particularly around the two local snack bar caravans.

THE BASICS

Distance: 4 miles / 6.5km

Gradient: Several easy slopes, one slightly stiffer than the rest

Severity: Easy

Approx. time to walk: 2 hours

Stiles: None, gates only

Maps: OS Landranger 177 (East London); Explorer 174 (Epping Forest and Lee Valley)

Path description: Woodland paths hard and grassy, the busy A104 has to be crossed, there and back

Start point: The parking area at High Beach, in Epping Forest (GR TQ 411982)

Parking: Dedicated roadside parking (IG10 4AE); often very busy at weekends. Limited bus service (check details; it could involve quite a long walk)

Dog friendly: Good for dogs, but will need to be on a lead crossing the A104

Public toilets: Adjacent to parking area

Nearest food: The King's Oak pub adjacent to the car park; two snack bars, one in a caravan and one in a hut, in the parking area

EPPING FOREST WALK

1. Facing the King's Oak pub turn right, for 75 yards up to the green gates on the right. Turn left along a faintly marked path, keeping direction parallel to the wooden fence on the left, to a junction with a more substantial path. Take note of this junction; it is not marked but you will need to recognise it on the return journey.

2. Take this track left to a triangular junction marked with a blue arrow marker post; bear right down the track which leads to the A104.

3. Cross this busy road with great care, go through the car park and bear right past a blue arrow marker post. Fork right and turn right at the next blue arrow and straight on past the final blue arrow; the track leads eventually to the road. Keep ahead, left of the first Strawberry Hill Pond and keep direction passing left of the second, larger pond, to where the track bears right to a wider grassier track.

Strawberry Hill Ponds are just a small part of the more than 100 ponds and lakes within the forest. Most are man-made, having been used as gravel pits; several are the result of World War II bombs and doodlebugs. All have been taken over by local wildlife and provide habitats for a wide range of species.

4. Take this track right, back to the A104 and again cross with care. Go through the narrow wooden gate and continue slight right on the substantial path to tarmac-covered Fairmead Road.

5. Turn right, to a white-topped post on the left; turn left along this wide clearing with the trees on the immediate left, to a junction with a more substantial track and turn right.

6. Follow this track to the road and cross; continue past the metal barrier opposite.

7. Keep on this track over the humps and through the dips to the unmarked junction at point 2, then turn left back to the road close to the 'King's Oak' and turn right, back to the car park.

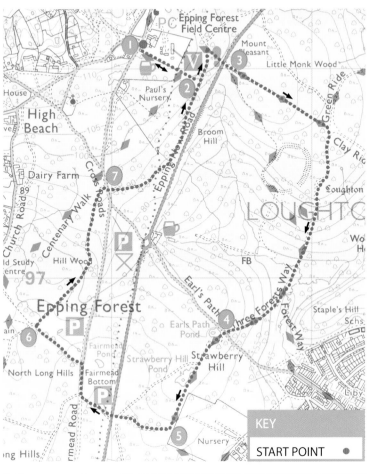

FINCHINGFIELD BROOK

FINCHINGFIELD, WITH ITS SPACIOUS VILLAGE GREEN COMPLETE WITH BABBLING BROOK THROUGH THE CENTRE, POPULATED BY FRIENDLY DUCKS AND SURROUNDED BY CHOCOLATE-BOX COTTAGES, IS PERHAPS ONE OF THE MOST ATTRACTIVE AND COMPREHENSIVELY PHOTOGRAPHED PLACES IN THIS COUNTRY. THE VILLAGE IS OFTEN CROWDED AND CAN BE FRAUGHT WITH PARKING DIFFICULTIES ON SUMMER WEEKENDS.

There is also a windmill, three thriving pubs, several tearooms, a shop, an impressive church and a historic 15th-century guildhall.

Finchingfield Brook, fed by several smaller streams as it approaches the village from the north, joins the River Pant at a confluence about a mile south of the village. The Pant continues to a point north of Braintree where it becomes the River Blackwater.

The village once had seven windmills; Duck End Mill is the last one standing. The building is owned by Essex County Council and open on the third Sunday of each month, between 2pm and 5pm. It is a post mill, where the whole mill building is manually turned to face the wind, by pushing a long pole. The whole structure rests on a substantial upright post which is supported by a massive trestle arrangement; this part was originally open until the roundhouse enclosing it was added in 1840. Specialists still argue as to the date of the mill's construction, indeed some historians believe that the mill was in use at some other location, dismantled and brought to the village to be reassembled. Inside the building, several dates from the mid-18th century have been inscribed in the woodwork, leading experts to the opinion that the mill was built around that time. The mill is sometimes referred to as Letch's Mill as it was run for most of the 19th century by various members of the Letch family.

The Grade I listed Guildhall was built around 1470 for the use of the Guild of the Holy Trinity, and also as a boys' school; an archway leads from the village through to the churchyard of St John the Baptist. The building fell into dereliction during the 20th century and it was not until 2011 that it was the subject of restoration. After completion in 2014 it now serves as a village heritage centre, library and museum. Volunteer staff are trained to bring to life the rich history of the village and the local area. There is also a facility for visiting children to dress in historical costume in order to experience a real understanding of bygone days.

THE BASICS

Distance: 3 miles / 4.8km

Gradient: Several easy slopes

Severity: Easy

Approx. time to walk: 1½ hours

Stiles: Two stiles and gates

Maps: OS Landranger 167 (Chelmsford); Explorer 195 (Braintree and Saffron Walden)

Path description: Grassy fields, hard paths, a not very busy road, field edges and wider hardcore farm roads. There is a section over a field which may be under cultivation and muddy in wet weather

Start point: One of the bridges over the brook in the centre of the village (GR TL 684328)

Parking: Sensible roadside parking in the village (CM7 4JX): it gets very busy on summer weekends; limited bus service (check details)

Dog friendly: Two stiles, not brilliant for dogs

Public toilets: None

Nearest food: Bosworth's tea room, Picture Pot tea room both on the green. Pubs the Three Tuns, the Red Lion and The Fox

FINCHINGFIELD BROOK WALK

1. Cross over the brook by the road bridge or the white-handrailed footbridge and go up the hill towards the church. Go past the Red Lion and turn left down a wide gap between two white houses; the right-hand house has some walls with pargeting on and black weatherboarding. At the marker disc at the left-hand end bear left between a lean-to garage and a fence, then continue along the path passing right of the mill to the high roadside path.

2. Turn right, across the three-sleeper footbridge under the willow tree and turn right at the signpost, down the field edge with the trees and the stream to the right, to the marker post on the right. Turn right across the field, which may be under cultivation although a path should be well marked within any crop, and cross the stile, then carry on between houses to the road.

3. Cross and take the road right to the Three Tuns and turn left, along the roadside path past the school to the footpath signpost on the left as the houses end. Turn left up the left-hand field edge into the corner; turn right and immediate left up steps. Keep direction on the path between fields left of the first telegraph pole; bearing right parallel to the telegraph poles and down to the road.

4. Turn right down to the junction and fork right, to the signpost at the corner. Keep left/ahead along the concrete farm road for 220 yards to an easily missed marker post on the right as the trees end. Turn right, down the track between fields and step over the stile at the corner. Continue direction with the hedge now right, down to the footbridge and cross over Finchingfield Brook.

5. Take the path right, between the fence and the brook; keep on the path and carry on through trees. The path goes between fences at the backs of the houses to a T-junction left of a footbridge. Turn left up this tarmac path to the road and then right along the roadside path back to the village centre.

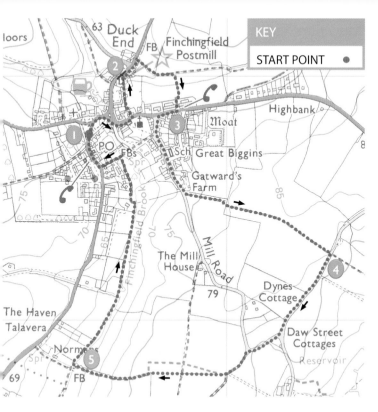

FLITCH WAY

THE ROMAN ROAD - STANE STREET RAN FROM ERMINE STREET NEAR BRAUGHING IN HERTFORDSHIRE TO THE ROMAN TOWN OF COLCHESTER. THE MODERN ROAD IS BELIEVED TO RUN ALONG THE COURSE OF THE ROMAN ROAD, AND IS NOW NUMBERED THE A120.

In 1869 a railway opened, parallel to Stane Street, between Bishop's Stortford and Braintree although this branch never realised its full potential, possibly because the proximity of the main road made it much more convenient to travel by bus. This was certainly the case throughout the years of the 20th century. Although excursion trains used the line until 1964, regular passenger traffic ceased in 1952, with freight services continuing through to 1972.

However during WWII the railway was very convenient for the transport of bombs, ammunition and other ordnance to the airfields close by. Several storage depots for explosives were built within Hatfield Forest, a suitable sparsely inhabited area with the trees providing camouflage and cover.

A lot of the trackbed of the railway at Great Dunmow has been utilised to take the B1256 road south avoiding the town centre. In 1989 most of the route of the dismantled railway became the Flitch Way path and cycleway, which has proved to be very popular with leisure walkers, cyclists and joggers.

Flitch Way is named for the local custom of awarding a flitch, or side of bacon, to any couple who have been married for more than a year and a day, who can prove that they have never had a cross word or fallen out. References are made to it in Geoffrey Chaucer's 'The Wife of Bath's Tale', where he assumes that the legend is so well known that he need not dwell on the details. It fizzled out in the middle of the 18th century but has since been rekindled with modern 'trials' being held every leap year.

Nearby Stansted Airport was constructed by the Royal Air Force during 1942; although officially RAF Stansted Mountfitchet it has always been referred to as just plain Stansted by military and civilian sources alike.

The base opened in August 1943 when it when it was used by the United States Air Force 344th Bombardment Group; flying the B-26 Martin Marauder bomber (see also Walk 15, Matching Green). Post war it was used to house German prisoners of war and for storage purposes. The runways were extended in the mid-1950s under a plan to transfer to NATO, but this was later cancelled. It finally came under civil control in 1957.

Holiday and charter flights started to use the airport and in 1966 it came under the control of the British Airports Authority who, in line with government policy, planned to develop Stansted into London's third airport. The first terminal opened in 1969. Further development prompted a public enquiry in 1984 which limited it to handling a maximum of 25 million passengers per year. The airport continues to grow an award-winning terminal which opened in 1991 is presently undergoing expansion, but Stansted lost its recent battle to construct a second runway.

THE BASICS

Distance: 3 miles / 5km

Gradient: Several easy slopes

Severity: Easy

Approx. time to walk: 1¼ hours

Stiles: None, gates only

Maps: OS Landranger 167 (Chelmsford); Explorer 195 (Braintree and Saffron Walden)

Path description: Woodland paths, hard paths and tarmac access road

Start point: Entrance car park, Hatfield Forest, pay and display, free for NT members (GR TL 547203)

Parking: As above (CM22 6NE). Bus service to Takeley (check details)

Dog friendly: Good for dogs

Public toilets: Further into the forest at the visitor centre

Nearest food: Further into the forest along the tarmac entry road at the visitor centre

FLITCH WAY WALK

1. Take the road away from the entrance through the gate and past the kiosk, turn right along the faint track in the grass parallel to the road and walk across the estate road. The track leads eventually to Flitch Way at the narrow metal gate.

2. Go through and turn left along the track of this dismantled railway, past the backs of the houses and parallel to the B1256 road leading out of Takeley. After three-quarters of a mile (1km) there is a wooden gate across the track; go past and there is a stile and two wooden gates one narrow and one wide. There is also a wooden gate on the right and a lane leading to the B1256.

3. Turn left and keep straight on, left of the first open area. Bear slight left on this main track, right of the open area on the left, leading to a fork where the main

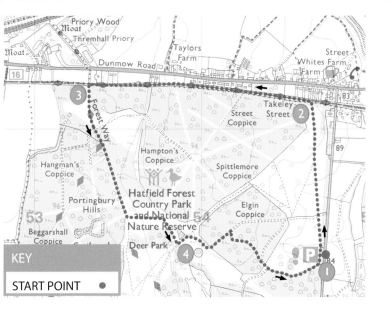

track goes right. Bear left on the narrower track over the wide wooden footbridge. Turn right and keep straight on to the road.

4. Take the main access road to the left, past the car park and turn right at the junction with the first exit sign; follow this road back to the entrance and the car park.

GREAT BARDFIELD

GREAT BARDFIELD SUPPORTED A COLONY OF ARTISTS BETWEEN 1930 AND 1970, AND DURING THE 1950S THEY HELD EXHIBITIONS IN THEIR OWN HOMES. THE EXHIBITIONS CAUGHT THE IMAGINATION OF PEOPLE INTERESTED IN ART, AND THOUSANDS OF PEOPLE VISITED THE SHOWS. THE EXHIBITIONS ALSO TOURED THE COUNTRY THROUGHOUT THE DECADE, BUT THE ARTISTIC COMMUNITY FADED AWAY WHEN MOST OF THE ARTISTS MOVED AWAY DURING THE 1960S.

Gibraltar Mill is now a private house. It is thought to have been built in 1704; experts believe that it was built on the site of a mill destroyed in the Great Storm of 1703. In 1899 the mill was badly damaged when it was tailwinded during a storm: the sails were torn off and the cap was broken. It was back in service by 1904 and worked until the death of the miller in 1930. A plan to demolish the mill was stopped by Essex County Council, but the internal machinery was all taken out when it was converted to living accommodation. In the 1987 hurricane the mill once again had a sail blown off.

Great Bardfield Watermill was in good condition until a catastrophic fire in 1993. Some of the machinery was salvaged, leaving some very sad-looking remains dominated by a rusty waterwheel. The 17th-century mill house was undamaged.

THE BASICS

Distance: 3¾ miles / 6km

Gradient: Several easy slopes

Severity: Easy

Approx. time to walk: 1¾ hours

Stiles: Two stiles and several gates

Maps: OS Landranger 167 (Chelmsford); Explorer 195 (Braintree and Saffron Walden)

Path description: Grassy fields, field edges, hard paths and wider hardcore farm roads. One section crosses a cultivated field and may be muddy in wet weather.

Start point: Brook Street near the grassy triangle junction, Great Bardfield (GR TL 677305)

Parking: Sensible roadside parking in the village (CM7 4RQ). Bus service (check for details)

Dog friendly: Yes, if they can manage stiles

Public toilets: None

Nearest food: Pubs in the village, The Vine and The Bell Inn, and tea room at the Blue Egg farm shop, Braintree Road

GREAT BARDFIELD WALK

1. Walk away from the village along Brook Street and Braintree Road, past the school and the Catholic Church to Bendlowes Road and turn left then immediate right, between metal barriers, up the path with trees either side. Keep straight on across the road and up the narrower path after the driveway swings left.

2. At the junction of tracks, take the wide farm road left with the hedge to the right, through the boundary to the marker post on the right. Turn right along the field edge with the tree and hedge to the right, through the boundary and past the right-hand hedge gap, all the way to the trees.

3. Turn left with the trees of Lodge Wood to the right, to the marker post and turn right, down the field edge and into the trees at the end. Take the more substantial track left through the edge of the trees, past the wide metal gate and bear right between the fence and the hedge to the road.

4. Cross and keep ahead/left downslope, to the footpath/signpost on the left. Cross a stile and take the track right and immediate left with the fence to the left. Turn right, over the wide concrete bridge at the marker disc on the gatepost and go around the field with the fence to the left into the far corner. Step over the hidden stile here.

5. Carry on parallel to the stream, over the metal handrailed footbridge. Keep ahead over the field which may be under cultivation although a path should be well marked within any crop. Go through the hedge gap and carry on with the hedge to the left and cross the stile at the end; the track in the grass is misleading as the stile is more to the right. Follow the path right of the pumping station and continue down the right-hand field edge with the hedge to the right. Go through the gap and up to the T-junction of tracks, and turn left.

6. The site of the watermill and the rusty remains of the waterwheel and some of the machinery is behind the mill house to the right. Go back to the T-junction and turn left from the original direction, then almost immediately right, over the concrete hardstanding and up the wide path between hedges and past the wide wooden gate to the hedge gap at the end on the left.

7. Go through and follow the path along the field edge which eventually leads to the right of the windmill. Turn right, down to the road and take the road right, back to the starting point.

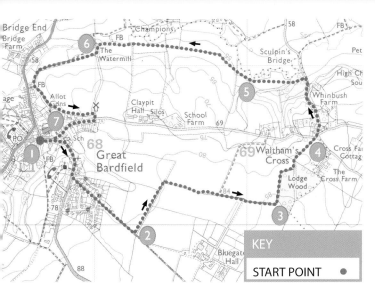

HADLEIGH CASTLE

WHEN HADLEIGH CASTLE WAS BUILT IN THE FIRST HALF OF THE 13TH CENTURY THE WATERS OF THE THAMES ESTUARY LAPPED THE BASE OF THE SLOPES BELOW. IT WAS BUILT BY HUBERT DE BERGH, EARL OF KENT AND THE KING'S JUSTICIAR.

Hubert had ruled the Kingdom during the minority of Henry III, who had been only nine years old when he ascended the throne, on the death of his father, King John, in 1216. During this time, war with France was always more than a possibility, and Henry granted Hubert a licence to build a castle on the high, steep slopes north of the Thames Estuary. It was unfortunately built on an unstable hill of clay and has suffered from subsidence ever since. Hubert enjoyed a prickly relationship with Henry; on his death in 1243 Henry took ownership of the castle.

The fortunes of the building ebbed and flowed, often reflecting the current state of relations with France. It also began to suffer damage to the building fabric as the land started to slide inexorably down the slope. During the 14th century over £2,000, a great deal of money at the time, was spent on the castle by King Edward III, who was almost constantly at war with France through his 50-year reign. From the beginning of the 15th century the importance of castles declined and by the middle of the 16th century the site was uninhabited and virtually derelict.

The ruins were sold to Sir Richard Rich, an avaricious Tudor courtier who made a profit on his purchase by selling any removable, useable stone. The only stone remaining is the rubble filling between the stronger outer walls. The site has since been a popular subject for a succession of artists. Critics have described a painting of the castle by Constable as 'one of his most monumental works'.

In 1891 the castle and surrounding land were bought by William Booth for the Salvation Army. He established a farm colony with the object of training disadvantaged Londoners in agricultural and rural trades, with a view to them using their skills in overseas colonies. The centre continues to train people with special educational needs in the farm and rare breeds centre. There is also a tea room/farm shop where home-made meals, snacks and produce may be purchased. The castle itself was given to the Ministry of Works in 1948 and is now looked after by English Heritage.

The country park was first proposed in 1970, but what was then known as Hadleigh Castle Country Park did not open until 1987. It is now a Site of Special Scientific Interest containing woodland, scrub grassland, salt marsh and tidal flats; ideal for the continued protection of mammals, birds, invertebrates and a considerable variety of flora. The 376-acre park is looked after by the Essex County Council Ranger Service. Hadleigh Farm and parts of the country park were the venue for the mountain biking events of the 2012 London Olympics.

THE BASICS

Distance: 3 miles / 5km

Gradient: A steep slope down and then back up again

Severity: Medium

Approx. time to walk: 1½ hours

Stiles: None, gates only

Maps: OS Landranger 178 (Thames Estuary); Explorer 175 (Southend-on-Sea and Basildon)

Path description: Gritty tracks, grassy paths, hard paths and wider hardcore access roads

Start point: Hadleigh Country Park, Chapel Lane, Benfleet, Southend (GR TQ 800869). Can also be started from Hadleigh Farm, Castle Lane, Benfleet, Southend (GR TQ 809864)

Parking: As above, pay and display at both locations (SS7 2PP or SS7 2AP). Bus service (check for details)

Dog friendly: Good for dogs

Public toilets: Yes, both locations

Nearest food: Salvation Army restaurants at both places

HADLEIGH CASTLE WALK

1. Take the path left of the play area and past both cattle grids. Keep on the lower path right, bearing left, with the trees to the right, over another cattle grid to a marker post marked 'PRIDE'. Turn right and zigzag down the gritty path, doubling back over the next cattle grid. Keep on this path through the green pinch barriers, across the track and through the wooden kissing gate. Follow the grass track ahead, downslope past the 'COURAGE' marker post and over the cattle grid.

2. Turn left, along the track with the fence and the hedge to the left. At a signpost the track joins the gritty path straight on (multi-use track) and carries on over a cattle grid. Keep direction on a left-hand field edge with a hedge to the left and the field to the right, to the signpost on the left; there is a farm road on the right just a few yards further on.

3. Go through the green kissing gate on the left and take the hardcore farm road upslope, passing left of the castle entrance. Keep straight on past the signpost. At this point the end of Southend pier may be seen to the east.

The well-known landmark stretching out $1^1/_3$ miles (2.25km) from Southend into the Thames Estuary dates from 1887. It replaced another mainly wooden structure built in 1830, which had been bought by Southend Council in 1873. The new pier was completed in 1889 and proved to be so popular that it was extended in 1897. The double-track, narrow-gauge electric railway built at the same time opened in 1890.

The pier has been subject to a series of unusual accidents and fires. In 1931 a man fell on to the track of the railway and was killed by a train. The pavilion at the shore end was destroyed by fire in 1959; about 500 people were trapped on the seaward side and had to be rescued by boats. The pavilion was replaced by a bowling alley, but the pier head suffered from a major fire in 1976 and the bowling alley burnt down in 1977. Economically, the resort and the pier were suffering from the effects of package holidays on the continent; the railway just needed too much money spending on repairs and maintenance and closed in 1978.

The council bowed to what they believed was inevitable and said the pier would have to close. However, protesters kept it open, finance was found and repairs were made in 1984/5; the railway was reduced to a single track with a passing place and new diesel powered trains were provided. Later that year a ship crashed into the structure, causing extensive damage that was temporarily repaired but not completed until 1989.

History repeated itself in 2005; the pier head which had been redeveloped in 2000 was destroyed in a fire which also badly damaged the railway. The end of the pier is now back to normal with the opening of a new pavilion in 2012.

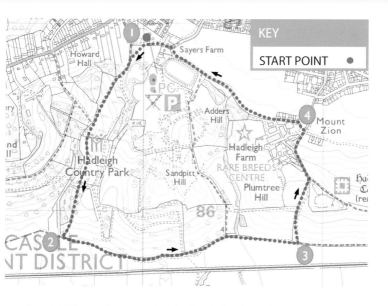

Bear right through the green pinch barriers to the signpost.

4. Turn left and bear right, then left past the front of the houses. Continue through the gap left of the barn ahead and follow the grit path back to the starting point and the car park.

HATFIELD FOREST

Hatfield Forest is a Site of Special Scientific Interest (SSSI) and a National Nature Reserve (NNR). It is owned by the National Trust and is a haven for all kinds of wildlife, flora and fauna. The name Hatfield does not mean it has a connection to the Hertfordshire town of the same name; Hatfield is one of this country's most popular names, derived from the Old English Hoep-Field; meaning heathland close to woodland.

A variety of trees are grown according to a woodland management system that has been practised for centuries. Some trees are coppiced, cut down to ground level and then allowed to regrow and pollarded, cut to head height to stop animals grazing on the young growth. These cuts are used in furniture, fencing, firewood and a million other things. Other trees are allowed to attain their full growth for use in large timber constructions like houses and boats.

The wide assortment of trees, flowers and plants support the life cycle of an equally wide range of birds, animals and invertebrates.

The word forest has come to mean an area densely packed with trees, but in its original form it was a large area of trees, heath and open scrubland ideal for hunting deer. The area had been owned by King Harold, but King William I took possession after the Conquest. It passed to his son Henry I, who designated it a Royal Hunting Forest, restricting its use by ordinary people. He introduced fallow deer and it was used extensively by royalty during the Norman era. King Henry III gave away the forest rights in 1238 and it passed through a succession of owners until 1729.

The Houblons were the descendants of Huguenots who had emigrated from Lille in 1560. They became wealthy and were involved in the establishment of the Bank of England. The family bought nearby Hallingbury Place and part of the forest in 1729. Jacob Houblon increased the area of forest he owned, and had the lake created and the Shell House built in 1746. In the 19th century the family began to favour the country house they owned in Berkshire and let the building to tenants during the early 20th century. However, in 1923 the house failed to find a new tenant and the whole property was put up for auction. The buyer was a timber merchant called Thomas Place who again could not find a buyer or tenant for the house; he demolished it in April 1924 and sold the materials for salvage.

Edward North Buxton (1840–1924) was a partner in a London brewery, a Member of Parliament and a member of a well-to-do Quaker family. He was a vociferous advocate of providing open and accessible land for the populations of large cities. He had already been involved in fighting for the future of Epping Forest, which was under threat from enclosure and further development. The forest was saved by its acquisition by the City of London. He also arranged for the purchase and reforestation of Hainault Forest, which had been stripped of all its trees by its previous owner.

In 1923 he learned that Hatfield Forest would probably be coming on to the market. He was very ill at the time and failed in his intention to buy it. However, his son Gerald purchased most of the forest from Thomas Place and the sale was completed on 8 January 1924; Buxton died the next day. Gerald gave the initial piece of land to the National Trust. The family were able to buy the rest of the forest to give to the Trust by the end of the year.

THE BASICS

Distance: 4¼ miles / 7.25km

Gradient: Flat

Severity: Easy

Approx. time to walk: 2 hours

Stiles: One stile and several gates

Maps: OS Landranger 167 (Chelmsford); Explorer 183 (Chelmsford and the Rodings) and 195 (Braintree and Saffron Walden)

Path description: Woodland paths, hard paths, a short section of not very busy road and tarmac access road

Start point: Entrance car park, Hatfield Forest, pay and display, free for NT members (GR TL 547203)

Parking: As above (CM22 6NE). Bus service to Takeley (check details)

Dog friendly: Yes, if they can manage the stile

Public toilets: Further into the forest at the visitor centre

Nearest food: Further into the forest along the tarmac entry road

HATFIELD FOREST WALK

1. Take the tarmac road into the trees around corners to the T-junction and turn left, past the first car park and follow the road over the bridge at the bottom of the valley. Bear right, left of the scrubby area, upslope and through the edge of the trees.

2. Turn right, up a wider path past the end of an even wider avenue (there is a post on the right with a yellow ring at the top). Continue ahead and turn sharp left, down the next wide avenue, where there is a yellow ringed marker post again. Keep on this track to the brick buildings at the end. Turn left to the National Trust sign, go through the narrow gate and keep direction between hedges.

3. Turn left, cross the stile and carry on along the path with the lake to the left. At the end bear right downslope and follow the hedged path over the footbridge to the barns. Carry on right of the barns, bearing right to a T-junction and turn left, keeping straight on when the tarmac surface ends. Bear left along this track between trees to the trees of Emblem's Coppice and turn right between the trees and the field. Continue over the two-plank footbridge, down to the corner and exit across the overgrown footbridge.

4. Turn left to the double signpost at the metal gates as the road bears right. Turn left through the gates and bear right away from the concrete tracks. Bear left between trees and further left, with trees to the left and open land to the right. Bear left along the track in the middle of the very wide avenue. Keep direction to where the clearing opens out on the left; there is a house here half hidden in the trees.

5. Bear right on the wide grass track to the Shell House car park. Continue along the hard path left of the buildings and right of the lake. Keep on the straight path and bear right of the boardwalk at the end.

6. Carry on along the path through the trees and then open ground nearly to the gates. Turn left and take the track in the grass leading back to the entrance car park.

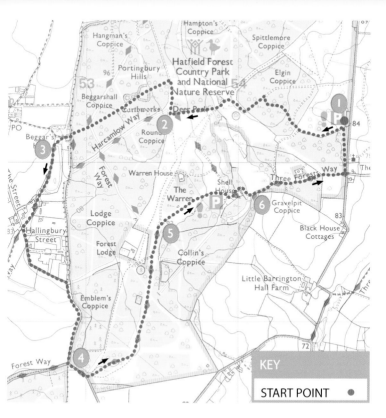

KEY

START POINT •

INGREBOURNE VALLEY

THE SOURCE OF THE INGREBOURNE RIVER LIES NEAR BRENTWOOD AND IT FLOWS SOUTH-WEST FOR 27 MILES (43.5 KM). THE RIVER CONTINUES THROUGH A FLOODPLAIN EAST OF HAROLD HILL AND THE OPEN LAND BETWEEN HORNCHURCH AND UPMINSTER. THE MARSHY LAND OF HORNCHURCH COUNTRY PARK IS FED BY THE RIVER, WHICH CARRIES ON TO THE THAMES AS RAINHAM CREEK.

The name is a combination of burn or bourne, meaning river, and Ing or Inga, the name of an individual landowner or a tribe. The Ingrebourne Valley is a Local Nature Reserve and the marshes are a Site of Special Scientific Interest (SSSI).

Hornchurch Country Park is the location of the Battle of Britain airfield RAF Hornchurch. The airfield first opened in 1915 with only two aircraft. The main threat in the early part of World War I was from airships. The first attack by a Hornchurch fighter on an airship took place on 13 October 1915, only ten days after the station opened, the airship escaped into clouds. The first airship was not brought down until nearly a year later, by Lieutenant William Leefe Robinson.

At the end of the war the airfield was closed, the buildings were demolished and the land went back to agricultural use. It was very quickly realised a mistake had been made and a brand new airfield, now called RAF Hornchurch, opened on the site in 1928.

The Hornchurch squadrons had been equipped with biplanes until January 1939 when the first Spitfires arrived. The station's position meant that fighters could be scrambled and intercept enemy aircraft as they approached London up the River Thames.

The first day of the Battle of Britain is usually agreed to be 8 July 1940; on that day a Hornchurch Spitfire brought down the first German fighter on to British soil. The battle was at its most intense from 13 August, named 'Eagle Day' by the Luftwaffe. Hornchurch was first bombed on 18 August and frequently after that. The Luftwaffe switched their attacks to London on 7 September, and suffered such grievous losses on the 15th that they started to believe that they could not defeat the RAF, and therefore the German Army could not invade.

The RAF presence at Hornchurch was increasingly scaled back in the post-war years; the station was used mainly for training and crew selection processes. It finally closed on 9 April 1962; it was quickly sold and most of the buildings were dismantled or demolished.

The Officer's Mess and Quarters which survive in the housing estate close by can easily be identified as former RAF buildings. Roads on the estate are named after pilots from the station and the local school is named after R. J. Mitchell, designer of the Spitfire. The eastern part of the airfield was the subject of an extensive gravel extraction process during the 1970s. When this had been completed the area was landscaped, becoming Hornchurch Country Park.

THE BASICS

Distance: 3¾ miles / 6km

Gradient: Flat

Severity: Easy

Approx. time to walk: 1¾ hours

Stiles: One stile and several gates

Maps: OS Landranger 177 (East London); Explorer 175 (Southend-on-Sea and Basildon)

Path description: Grassy fields, field edges, hard paths and wider hardcore access roads

Start point: The car park at Hornchurch Country Park, Squadrons Approach, Hornchurch (GR TQ 536849)

Parking: As above (RM12 6TS). Bus service (check for details)

Dog friendly: One stile but not adapted for dogs

Public toilets: At visitor centre

Nearest food: At the restaurant on site

1. Walk away from the car park, passing left of the white barriers. and continue along the path to the right of the trees. Keep on this track with the trees to the left, for three quarters of a mile (1km), passing right of Albyns Farm.

2. Turn left along the wide track with the farm buildings still left, past the large metal gate. Follow the track left and continue with the trees to the left to the signpost for Berwick Woods. The small round concrete installations are extremely rare Tett Turrets, named

after their inventor, a man called Tett. It was prefabricated, very cheap and very simple; a standard length of 4-foot concrete pipe contained a machine gun in a concrete turret which revolved on ball bearings. It had considerable drawbacks, the main one being access, which was only through the open top. One well-placed grenade and it would have been finished.

3. Turn right, over the substantial footbridge across the Ingrebourne River, and carry on along this wide path with the trees of Berwick Woods to the right, to the black barriers at the corner of a road.

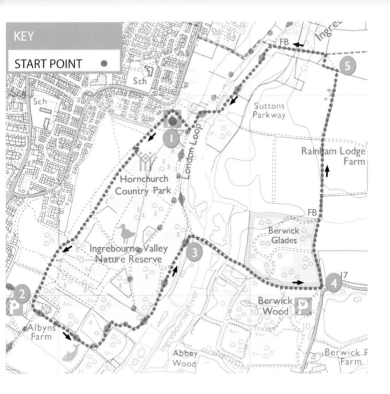

KEY

START POINT ●

4. Take the track left, between two large lumps of stone, with the more open Berwick Chase now on the left. Continue direction over the footbridge and up the right-hand field edge with the hedge to the right; straight on over the crossroads of tracks. Keep ahead and cross the footbridge/stile at the signpost in the hedge gap.

5. Turn left, on the path with the hedge left and bear right into the trees and then left with the track over the substantial footbridge back across the Ingrebourne River to the four-way signpost. Turn left and follow the path back to the car park.

LAYER MARNEY TOWER

HENRY, 1ST LORD MARNEY WAS HENRY VIII'S LORD PRIVY SEAL. HE INTENDED THE NEW HOUSE HE STARTED TO BUILD IN AROUND 1520 TO RIVAL THE OTHER GREAT TUDOR PALACE AT HAMPTON COURT. HE HAD SEEN ONLY AN IMPRESSIVE GATEHOUSE, A BRICK-BUILT CHURCH AND SOME OTHER ANCILLARY BUILDINGS FINISHED BEFORE HE DIED IN 1523. HIS SON INTENDED TO SEE THE PROJECT THROUGH TO COMPLETION BUT DIED ONLY TWO YEARS LATER, LEAVING NO CHILDREN.

The tower has been cleverly designed to make it seem bigger than it actually is. At first glance it appears to be eight stories high, but each floor has two windows, one on top of the other. It is not an optical illusion but a very effective trick on the subconscious.

The building reflected the belief at the time that the bigger, more costly and flamboyant one's house, the more important the owner. At 80 feet (24m) it is the tallest Tudor gatehouse, with 99 steps to the top of the tower. Built of brick mixed with black-glazed bricks in a form of decoration called diapering, there is further decoration made of terracotta. Although the crenellations are also only decorative as the house was never meant to be a fortress, Marney still had to obtain special permission from the king to include them in his design.

On 22 April 1884 the Great Colchester Earthquake struck the area. Measuring around 4.6 on the Richter Scale and with an epicentre situated between Wivenhoe and Abberton, the earthquake caused massive damage to buildings in a wide area south and south-east of Colchester, and the church at Virley was almost totally destroyed. Layer Marney Tower was badly damaged and experts believed it was irreparable. Brother and sister Alfred and Kezia Peach took on the expensive job, which was continued by Walter de Zoete, who left the tower with an interior more Edwardian than Tudor.

Gerald and Susan Charrington fell in love with the tower after their marriage in the adjacent church in 1957. They bought the property in 1959 and it has remained in their family ever since.

THE BASICS

Distance: 4½ miles / 7.25km

Gradient: Several easy slopes

Severity: Easy

Approx. time to walk: 2¼ hours

Stiles: Two and several gates

Maps: OS Landranger 168 (Colchester); Explorer 184 (Colchester)

Path description: Grassy fields and farm roads, field edges and wider hardcore farm roads. There is also a section of not very busy road and some short pieces of cultivated field, which may be muddy in wet weather

Start point: An unsurfaced lay-by on a corner of the B1022, north-east of Tiptree (GR TL 922187). The walk may also be started from the Layer Marney Tower car park (GR TL 928176)

Parking: An unsurfaced layby on a corner of the B1022, as above, north-east of Tiptree (CO5 9XG). Or the car park (pay and display) at the Tower (CO5 9US), as above. On a bus route (check times)

Dog friendly: A couple of stiles, not really suitable for dogs

Public toilets: None

Nearest food: At Layer Marney Tower or in Tiptree (two miles)

1. Facing the road, turn left along the grass verge to the hedge gap on the left just before the bus stop. Turn left along the wide, mown path in the grass, to the road; carefully take the road left, past the junction to the small lay-by on the corner where the road swings right.

2. Step over the stile in the corner and keep ahead down the wide, fenced path, through the wide gap at the end. Bear left across this field, which may be under cultivation although a path should be well marked within any crop, to the signpost in the hedge gap. Cross the footbridge and go on to the road.

3. Take the road right, down to the junction and the signpost just beyond; turn left along the gravel drive left of the house and continue straight on up the field edge with the hedge to the left. As the field edge veers right, bear left across a footbridge with metal pipe handrails. Carry on between the hedge and the fence to a three way signpost.

4. Turn right, signposted to the church, and left through the hedge gap, into the churchyard. Go through, passing right of the church and out of the gate. Turn left along the stony driveway to the road and turn left, upslope to the signpost on the right. Turn right, upslope on the path between fields. Go through the gap at the end and bear left to the road.

5. Turn left, up to the top where the road turns left and turn right through the gate and into the field. Take a diagonal to the farm track on the far side and turn right, with the hedge to the left, to the far left corner. Follow the track left and right and continue on the left-hand field edge, through the gap in the corner and along the path between the fence and the hedge to the road. Turn left on the road through the houses of Birch Green village to the footpath signpost at the end.

6. Take the gravel drive left, passing right of the houses, past the wide metal gate. Keep on this wide stony track parallel to the power lines, around a double bend and carry on slightly left at the reservoir to where the main track bears left at the far corner of the reservoir.

7. Go through the kissing gate on the right and keep the original direction through the kissing gates and over the footbridge to the road. Cross and keep straight on,

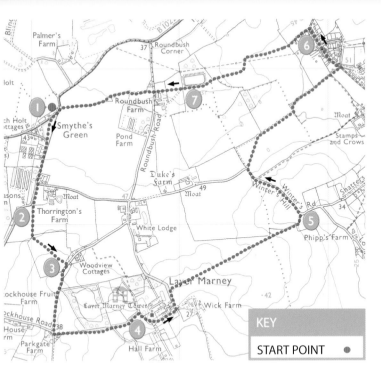

down steps and over the stile; carry on up the right-hand field edge between the hedge and the fence and over the stile footbridge in the corner. Turn left along the left-hand field edge with the hedge to the left all the way to the road. The lay-by and starting point is just to the left.

LOG CHURCH

ST ANDREW'S IN GREENSTED IS A CHURCH BUILT FROM SPLIT LOGS, AND WAS BELIEVED FOR MANY YEARS TO BE THE OLDEST WOODEN CHURCH IN THE WORLD AND POSSIBLY THE OLDEST WOODEN BUILDING IN EUROPE. THE CHURCH IS NOT ALL THAT WELL KNOWN BUT IT WILL BE VERY FAMILIAR TO PHILATELISTS.

Sted or stead is an Old English word meaning place, so the name Greensted literally means 'green village'. The name of the village has been shortened in recent years from the more difficult Greensted-juxta-Ongar, which was originally used to differentiate the village from the other Greenstead in Essex. The village is now more often referred to as just plain Greensted; the juxta comes from 'juxtapose' (put next to), a word which itself seems to be used very little today.

As with many older buildings it is difficult to be exact about age, but Greensted is thought to have been the site of a holy building for as long as there has been Christianity in England. While archaeologists were investigating the church in the 1960s they discovered evidence of timber buildings predating the present church. These experts originally identified the logs as having been cut in the middle of the ninth century. This is now in dispute and more modern dating methods have fixed the date at the middle of the 11th century. A possibly apocryphal tale tells of the body of St Edmund, the Saxon king killed by the Danes in 870, resting in the church overnight on its way to be reinterred in Bury St Edmunds. However, other stories tell of St Edmund being reburied a hundred years before this.

The nave, the oldest part of the church, is built in a traditional Saxon style with split oak tree trunks. This style makes the building a palisade church. The logs are piled into the ground or attached to a sill foundation, with the rounded edge facing the outside. These logs were load bearing and the roof was built on top of them. It has been the subject of a constant stream of rebuilding and updating ever since. The chancel, originally built in the same manner as the main church, was replaced by a brick structure in the 16th century and the spire-topped tower was added during the 17th century. The Victorians seemed unable to resist rebuilding churches whether they needed it or not and they reroofed the building and put in six dormer windows in place of the original three. They also rebuilt the porch.

In 1972, as part of a series celebrating British architecture, the Post Office issued a set of stamps illustrating five iconic churches. The lowest 3p denomination (3p to post a letter?) showed a painting of St Andrew's Church.

THE BASICS

Distance: 4½ miles / 7.25km

Gradient: Some easy slopes

Severity: Easy

Approx. time to walk: 2¼ hours

Stiles: Several stiles and gates

Maps: OS Landranger 167 (Chelmsford); Explorer 183 (Chelmsford and the Rodings)

Path description: Grassy fields, roadside paths, field edges and wider hardcore farm roads

Start point: The car park close to the library in Chipping Ongar (GR TL 552031)

Parking: As above (CM5 9AR). On a bus route (check details)

Dog friendly: A couple of stiles, not really suitable for dogs

Public toilets: Adjacent to car park

Nearest food: Restaurants, cafés, pubs and takeaways close by

LOG CHURCH WALK

1. Go to the High Street and turn right, through the town to the junction with the Borough. Cross to the opposite pavement and turn right past the Two Brewers, bearing left upslope on Greensted Road to the first footpath signpost.

2. Bear left up this hardcore track with the school to the right, and carry on between trees to the marker post on the right. Bear right, parallel with the power lines over this field which may be under cultivation although a track should be well marked within any crop. Cross the footbridge in the hedge gap.

3. Continue ahead up the left-hand field edge with the trees and the dyke to the left. The path passes right of two small ponds and bears right at a marker post, with the trees and the dyke still left, and cross the footbridge at the end. Carry on along the right-hand field edge with the trees and the hedge now on the right, over the two-sleeper bridge in the corner. Take the footpath slightly left, left of the tree – a track should be well marked – and go through the trees to the road.

4. Keep ahead through the gate opposite, down the fenced path and turn right to the stile. Cross and bear right, through the boundary at the corner and up the next field edge with the trees to the right. Keep round the edge to the yellow-top marker post and take the path right, through trees to the road.

5. Turn left and immediately right, up the path between the hedge and the fence to a yellow-top post at the end. Turn right, across the field to a yellow-top post at a narrow metal gate, then follow the track through trees. At the next metal gate turn right on a wider path to a marker post, then turn left through a wooden kissing gate.

6. Keep direction through the pinch stiles into the enclosed path which leads through a kissing gate to the field edge. Turn right with the hedge to the right up to the road.

7. Cross and follow the path on the field edge bearing slightly right to the footbridge at the end. Cross and walk up the double concrete driveway to the Log Church.

8. After looking at the church go back out of the churchyard gate and turn left. Take the wide tarmac drive to the left and go through the narrow gate at the end, and walk down the left-hand field edge with the trees to the left. Keep direction over the footbridge and up the path between fields. Continue straight on up the road into Chipping Ongar to find the car park and the starting point.

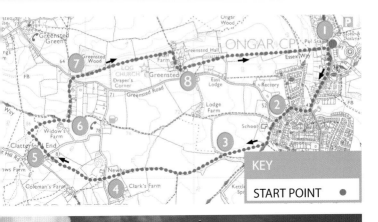

MATCHING GREEN

MATCHING GREEN HAS ONE OF THE LARGEST VILLAG[E]
GREENS IN ESSEX AT NEARLY 14 ACRES (6.5 HECTARES). IT I[S]
SURROUNDED BY INTERESTING AND QUIRKY COTTAGES AN[D]
HAS RESIDENT DUCKS IN A SMALL POND.

The village is spread over a very wide area; historically the church at Matching, about a mile away, is the centre of the village. Standing next to the church is the Marriage Feasting Hall, a Tudor style two-storey timber-framed building, said to have been built in 1480 although it has a host of more modern 19th/20th-century alterations. It is said to have been built 'for the entertainment of poor people on their wedding day' but has also been used as a schoolroom and an almshouse.

The other larger part of the village is Matching Tye, mainly residential and complemented by the Fox Inn. Several other widely spaced, outlying settlements complete the village.

To the east of Matching Green is the site of the Second World War airfield RAF Matching[.] United States Air Force Martin B-26 Marauder twin-engine bombers arrived durin[g] January 1944. They flew their first mission on 15 February, and completed another 15[0] before moving to airfields in France after D-Day. The B-26 was an unpopular aircraft tha[t] crashed far too often, giving its crews cause to nickname it 'The Widowmaker' or mor[e] pointedly the Martin Murderer. The Royal Air Force used Matching for the rest of the war[,] flying Douglas C-47 Skytrains (Dakotas) for the training of paratroops. The airfield returne[d] to agricultural use very quickly after closure in 1946. The control tower still stands an[d] some of the narrow perimeter roads are used for farming access. Some of the hangar[s] were dismantled and re-erected at North Weald, and are now used by a TV productio[n] company.

THE BASICS

Distance: 4½ miles / 7.6km

Gradient: Flat

Severity: Easy

Approx. time to walk: 2¼ hours

Stiles: Two stiles and gates

Maps: OS Landranger 167 (Chelmsford); Explorer 183 (Chelmsford and the Rodings)

Path description: Grassy fields, hard paths, field edges and wider hardcore farm roads. A couple of sections cross fields which may be under cultivation and will be muddy in wet weather

Start point: The Chequers pub on the village green (GR TL 535110)

Parking: Sensible roadside parking at the side of the village green (CM17 0PZ); there is no parking on the green. Limited bus service (check details)

Dog friendly: Two stiles, but not adapted for dogs

Public toilets: None

Nearest food: The Chequers pub as above

1. Cross the green and walk along the road towards Matching Tye to the footpath signpost on the almost immediate right; turn right along this path between hedges. Turn left, into the corner and right, along the field edge with the hedge to the left, to the marker post at the top left corner.

2. Take the tarmac driveway left, to the yellow-topped marker post at Brick House. Bear right, then left to the marker post and take the track between fields to the right. Follow this track left to the yellow-top post right of the clump of trees. Bear right across the open field, which may be under cultivation although a path should be well marked within any crop, and step over the stile.

3. Continue ahead up the slightly rising field edge through the kissing gate at the top and turn left along the tarmac driveway passing left of the church. Turn right along the track between fences into a dip and up the other side to a marker post. Turn left on this field edge with the hedge and the dyke to the left, all the way to the road at Matching Tye.

4. Turn left to the junction at the Fox Inn in the village centre. Bear right, along the roadside path to the road on the left signposted to Carter's Green. Turn left and follow the road right, then left to a wide metal gate on the left, just before the right-hand corner. Take the wide farm track right and left through the farmyard and the gap to the field.

5. Turn left, with the dyke and then the trees of Matching Park to the left. As the trees end turn right, to the marker post, and left, through the field boundary to the road. Turn right, to the concrete signpost, and take the field edge right; carry on left and right, to the far marker post and turn left over the footbridge.

6. Keep straight on over the field – a path should be visible through any crop – and continue straight on along the field edge, with the trees to the left. Bear slight left where a track should still be visible, and again straight on up the left-hand field edge. Cross the footbridge and carry on through the next field, past a stile and bear right to the road in Matching Green. Turn left to the village centre and the green and right back to the starting point at the The Chequers.

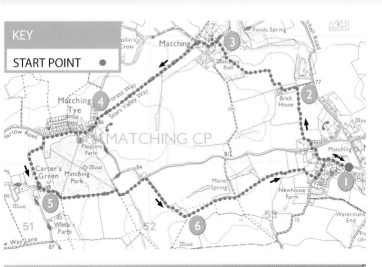

KEY

START POINT ●

PAPER MILL LOCK

THE RIVER CHELMER AT PAPER MILL LOCK HAS BEEN CANALISED SINCE THE END OF THE 18TH CENTURY. THE RIVER RISES BETWEEN DEBDEN GREEN AND THAXTED. IT FLOWS AROUND THE EASTERN SIDE OF GREAT DUNMOW, THEN SOUTH EAST AND SOUTH TO CHELMSFORD AND A CONFLUENCE WITH THE RIVER CAN. THE RIVER TURNS EAST WHERE IT BECOMES THE CHELMER AND BLACKWATER NAVIGATION. THE WATERWAY CONTINUES EAST TO JOIN THE BLACKWATER ESTUARY EAST OF MALDON.

Plans to canalise the river had first been promoted in 1677 but finance was always an issue. A plan passed in 1766 failed because money could not be raised in time. The town and port of Maldon normally opposed these plans on commercial grounds, but in the end the Act of Parliament authorising the work was passed. This solved the problem by going around the town to a new basin at  Heybridge Port east of Maldon. The Chelmer and Blackwater Navigation, built between 1793 and 1797, runs from the centre of Chelmsford close to its confluence with the River Can for 14 miles (22.5km). During that journey it descends 75 feet (23m) at Beeleigh, joins the River Blackwater and skirts the northern edge of Maldon.

Trade on the Navigation peaked at 60,000 tons of cargo per year in the middle of the 19th century; mainly coal on its way in and grain on its way out. A wharf close to Paper Mill Lock handled cargo for Little Baddow. Two mills stood close to the lock when it was first built, one for grinding grain for bread while more unusually the other ground chemicals for paper production.

The location was often used as a halfway overnight stop for the barge crews, who could bed down for the night in a nearby bunkroom, with the horses being stabled in what is now the tearoom. The canal was not as badly affected as some by the coming of the railways as there was never a direct railway connection between Chelmsford and Maldon. However, traffic and revenues declined through the first part of the 20th century and the last commercial voyage took place in 1972. The navigation is unusually still owned by the original company, as it was not nationalised with the rest of the canals in 1948.

The company allowed pleasure boats on the route after 1972, but were still unable to make the canal pay. British Waterways were not interested in taking over so the canal is now operated by the Inland Waterways Association, a charity that campaigns for the use, maintenance and restoration of all of Britain's inland waterways.

THE BASICS

Distance: 5½ miles / 8.8km

Gradient: One easy slope down and then back up

Severity: Easy

Approx. time to walk: 3 hours

Stiles: Several stiles and gates

Maps: OS Landranger 167 (Chelmsford); Explorer 183 (Chelmsford and the Rodings)

Path description: Grassy fields, field edges, river bank and wider hardcore farm roads. There is also a section across a field which may be under cultivation and possibly muddy in wet weather

Start point: The General's Arms' pub, The Ridge, Little Baddow (GR TL 781072)

Parking: Sensible roadside parking in the village (CM3 4SX). Limited bus service (check details)

Dog friendly: Yes, if they can manage stiles

Public toilets: None

Nearest food: The General's Arms and the The Rodney Inn. Tea room at the Paper Mill Lock

PAPER MILL LOCK WALK

1. Go up to the crossroads and take Spring Elms Lane to the right, to the signpost on the left, then go down this gravel driveway bearing left of the white house. Go through the gap between the fence and the trees into Heather Hills Nature Reserve. Keep on the path ahead and continue straight on at the signpost, with the trees to the left and the field to the right, to the fence at the bottom. Turn right, along the field edge and go through the gap in the corner. Take the wide track left, passing right of the houses, and continue to the road.

2. Cross and keep ahead, between fields with the dyke to the left, down to the trees at the bottom. Turn right, along the field edge with the trees to the left, bearing left to the River Chelmer. Turn left along the path on the river bank with the river to the right, all the way to the road at Paper Mill Bridge and cross this surprisingly busy road carefully.

3. Go through the gate and keep on the path between the tearoom and Paper Mill Lock; follow the path ahead with the river still right, past the marker post on the left (half a mile or nearly 1km) to the signpost just before a blue handrailed footbridge (three-quarters of a mile (1km)). Go through the gap and cross the field ahead, up the slight slope (this field may be under cultivation although a path should be well marked within any crop), passing right of the church. Go down the steps to the road.

4. Turn left the short distance to the signpost at the road entry on the right. Go past the stile and the marker disc, bearing left past the brick farm building, to a junction at a telegraph pole. Keep left then right, past another telegraph pole. Keep direction on this hardcore farm road and then the wide grass track between the fence and the hedge to an easily missed gap in the hedge marked by a disc.

5. Turn left across this field and over a stile; carry on up the path between trees to the road. Turn right, past the white house to the signpost on the left; step over the stile and take the narrow path between the hedge and the fence. Continue through a metal kissing gate past the substantial fence on the right to a junction of wide tracks.

6. Turn right to a marker post with a double yellow arrow and take this narrow path left. Bear right at the junction past the back of a school and join the driveway ahead, bearing left to a tarmac surface and a marker post. Bear right and follow this driveway left to the road. Turn left along the roadside path, past the General's Arms to the crossroads.

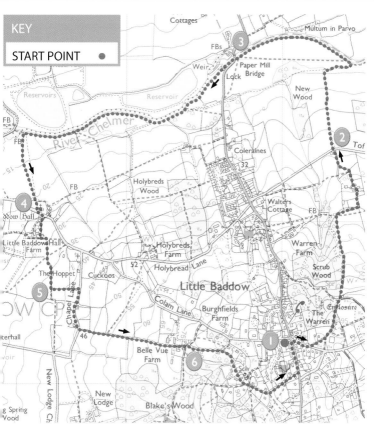

KEY

START POINT ●

THE RIVER RODING RISES EAST OF DUNMOW AND FOLLOWS A GENERALLY SOUTHWARD COURSE THROUGH THE COUNTY OF ESSEX TO THE THAMES AT CREEKMOUTH. THE LAST TIDAL SECTION OF THE RIVER IS USUALLY REFERRED TO AS BARKING CREEK.

Chipping is a fairly common prefix to English place names, and is derived from the Old English Ceping, meaning marketplace. The Ongar section of the name means grassland.

The Heritage Railway line based in Chipping Ongar has quite a chequered history. It started in 1865 as an extension to the Great Eastern Railway suburban line from Loughton, though most trains terminated at Epping. Some rationalisation took place within the London railway lines following the nationalisation of the railways in 1948. The London Passenger Transport Board (LPTB or just London Transport) took over the railway from British Railways. The line was then electrified and became part of the Underground Central Line; however, the electrification stopped at Epping as it was not thought to be commercially viable to carry on to Chipping Ongar. A shuttle service operated by steam engines ran until 1957 when the line was at last electrified. It was unfortunately done on the cheap, and the voltage drop meant that only four-car trains could use the route, again with a shuttle service. The section was never very strong commercially and since Chipping Ongar was now classified as green belt, very little housing development had taken place. In 1981 London Transport shut an intermediate

station at Blake Hall, saying that only six people used it. The whole section was finally closed in 1994, with every journey costing the company £7 more than the ticket price.

The line was, however, of great interest to railway preservation societies, as it was almost a 'going concern'. In 1998 it reopened for a service run by preserved diesel trains, but closed again from 2007 to 2012 so that major engineering and signalling works could take place, enabling the line to use steam engines again. It now operates on weekends and bank holidays.

The castle dates from the early Norman era. It was a simple motte and bailey; an earthen mound called a motte which had a stone keep on top, surrounded by a fortified curtain wall called a bailey, and encircled by a wide moat. The stonework was replaced by a brick residence which has itself been knocked down, and only the bare mound survives, covered in undergrowth and trees. The site is not open to the general public.

THE BASICS

Distance: 6 miles / 9.5km

Gradient: Some easy slopes

Severity: Easy

Approx. time to walk: 3 hours

Stiles: Several stiles and gates

Maps: OS Landranger 167 (Chelmsford); Explorer 183 (Chelmsford and the Rodings)

Path description: Grassy fields, roadside paths, field edges and wider hardcore farm roads

Start point: The car park close to the library in Chipping Ongar (GR TL 552031)

Parking: As above (CM5 9AR). On a bus route (check details)

Dog friendly: Yes, if they can manage stiles

Public toilets: Adjacent to car park

Nearest food: Restaurants, cafés, pubs and takeaways close by

RODING VALLEY WALK

1. Cross over High Street from the car park and turn left along the roadside path, back towards the A414. At Love Lane on the right, turn right, past a signpost and the wide wooden gate; carry on up the tarmac path between the fence and the hedge and the left-hand side of the playing field. Go through the corner and turn left and immediate right, down the slight slope with the hedge to the right, to the marker post on the right.

2. Bear left across the field to a marker post at a wide hedge gap; it may be better if the field is under cultivation to walk into the corner and take the field edge left to the marker post. Go through and turn left, with the hedge to the left, up to where the trees on the right end. Bear right and go through the gap and up the steps to the road. Cross this busy road carefully and continue down the steps the other side; follow the path right, then bear left over the stile at the metal gate.

3. Keep ahead over the road, past the gate, and bear right past the marker post at the corner. Turn left and keep on this track with the hedge to the left, over the fence and the footbridge in the hedge ahead. Keep ahead – there are often high nettles here – over the footbridge at the far right, along the path and across the next footbridge. Carry on over the third footbridge and up the left-hand field edge with the River Roding to the right, bearing right then left to a footbridge.

4. Take the path straight on with the river close by to the right for a mile, all the way to the long metal handrailed footbridge and cross to the right (beware of the missing plank).

5. Bear right, to the marker post at the hedge corner. and take the field edge right, with the hedge to the left, over the footbridge at the far left. Keep straight on over the field ahead which may be under cultivation although a path should be well marked within any crop.

6. Continue along the field edge with the trees to the right and maintain direction on the wide double track through the trees. Carry on between the buildings at Little Forest Hall along the concrete farm road to the marker post just past the Little Forest Hall Cottages. Keep straight on across the field (a track should again be well marked) and rejoin the concrete road close to West Park Lodge.

7. Bear right, through an overgrown and easily missed hedge gap and along the left-hand field edge. As this track ends at a corner, carry on ahead over the field on a path which should be clearly seen, over stiles to the A414 road.

8. Cross this busy road carefully and go over the stile, then bear slight left across the field, through the fenced path right of the pub, into High Ongar village, turn right

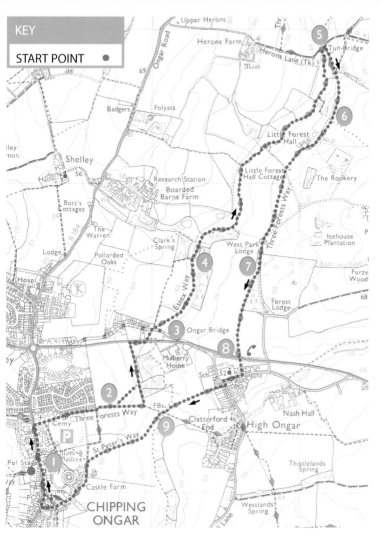

along the roadside path to the junction and left, the short distance to the signpost on the right. Turn right, along the wide track with the wall to the left through the kissing gate and down between fields to the river.

9. Cross the high footbridge and turn left along the river bank, bear right, left of the dead tree; go through the hedge gap here and cross the field (a track should be visible) to the boundary. Take the track left and bear left and right between the hedge and the fence. Continue to the road and keep straight on to the High Street. Turn right, through the town back to the car park.

STISTEDHALL PARK

THE RIVER BLACKWATER RISES AS THE RIVER PANT JUST EAST OF SAFFRON WALDEN. IT FLOWS EAST AND SOUTH-EAST TO BOCKING, A NORTHERN SUBURB OF BRAINTREE, WHERE IT CHANGES TO THE BLACKWATER. THE RIVER CONTINUES EAST PAST COGGESHALL AND SOUTH PAST KELVEDON AND WITHAM TO THE BLACKWATER ESTUARY WHERE IT IS JOINED BY THE RIVER CHELMER.

Stisted Hall is now a care home marketed as Prince Edward Duke of Kent Court. The hall was built in 1825, close to what was the original stately home of the Savill-Onley family.

The Golf Club came to Stistedhall Park in 1973. The club had to move as the Braintree Bypass was being constructed across its original course.

All Saints Church used to be classed as a 'peculiar', a very descriptive label. It meant that the church belonged in another diocese rather than the one in which it was geographically located. The estate of Stisted Hall had originally belonged to the monks of Canterbury Cathedral; at the reformation the property was sold on but the church remained under Canterbury's jurisdiction until 1845. It was briefly part of the Middlesex diocese, but since 1895 has been in its natural position as part of the See of Chelmsford.

THE BASICS

Distance: 2¼ miles / 3.6km

Gradient: One easy slope

Severity: Easy

Approx. time to walk: 1¼ hours

Stiles: One stile and several gates

Maps: OS Landranger between 167 (Chelmsford) and 168 (Colchester); Explorer 195 (Braintree and Saffron Walden)

Path description: Grassy fields, riverbank, woodland paths, golf course and a not very busy road

Start point: All Saints Church, The Street, Stisted (GR TL 799246)

Parking: Roadside parking in the village (CM77 8AP)

Dog friendly: If they can manage the stile and several gates

Public toilets: None

Nearest food: The Onley Arms, Stisted

STISTEDHALL PARK WALK

1. Take the path with paving slabs in the grass away from the village, through the kissing gate to the marker post at the churchyard corner. Turn left carefully, watching for golf balls, across the fairway, then right, down the edge of the golf course with the trees to the left to the bottom corner.

2. Turn right, past the marker post, with China Bridge off to the left, along the bank of the River Blackwater. Pass right of the wide wooden bridge and bear right, upslope with the trees to the left, to the tarmac driveway. Take the drive left between gateposts to the road. Turn right and walk carefully along the side of this not very busy road, then at the top follow the road right to the first signpost.

3. Turn left across the concrete area, passing between gateposts, and continue along the path through trees. The path bears right and eventually left to a T-junction of tracks next to a dyke; turn right and go through the corner. Bear right between the fence and the hedge and go over the stile on the right.

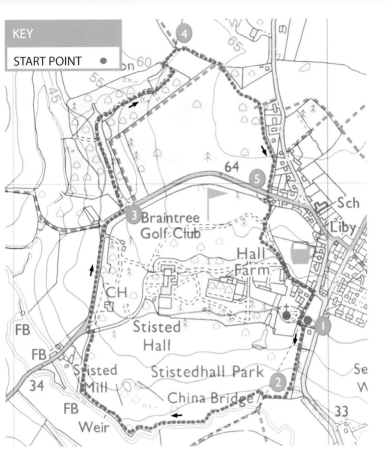

4. Cross the footbridge to the right and keep ahead on the right-hand field edge with the trees to the right, through the narrow gap in the corner to the marked barriers on the right. Go through and take the path left, along the edge of the golf course, to a marker post. Keep straight on, passing right of the next marker post, along the track through trees at the backs of the houses. Continue through the grass and the hedge gap to the road.

5. Turn right and immediately left to a marker post, and take the path left between fences and follow it to the right. Bear left with the path, past the ninth tee and follow the obvious path through trees past a marker post, then keep ahead on a stony driveway which leads to the road. Turn right, back to the church gate and the starting point.

STOUR ESTUARY

THE SOURCE OF THE RIVER STOUR IS CLOSE TO THE VILLAGES OF WESTON COLVILLE, WESTON GREEN AND WEST WRATTING IN SOUTH CAMBRIDGESHIRE (SOUTH OF NEWMARKET). IT FLOWS EAST AND SOUTH EAST PAST HAVERHILL AND SUDBURY, THEN THROUGH CONSTABLE COUNTRY; THE AREA OF OUTSTANDING NATURAL BEAUTY (AONB) DEDHAM VALE. FOR MOST OF ITS COURSE IT FORMS THE BORDER BETWEEN SUFFOLK AND ESSEX; IT ENTERS THE WIDE STOUR ESTUARY AT MANNINGTREE TO ITS MOUTH AT HARWICH WHERE IT IS BRIEFLY JOINED BY THE RIVER ORWELL.

A joint stock company was set up in 1705 to make the river navigable from Sudbury to Manningtree. It raised £4,800 to 'cut and manage' the river. Lighters (unpowered barges) were still being used on the Navigation until World War II. The River Stour Trust was formed in 1968 with the intention of reopening the waterway between Sudbury and the sea. The trust has successfully restored locks further up the river but the head of navigation is still at Manningtree.

The estuary is a haven for a various species of wildlife, particularly ducks and geese. A bird seen in increasingly large numbers is the little egret, a member of the heron family; snowy white in colour and just slightly smaller than a grey heron. The bird was a very rare visitor to England until this century.

Manningtree claims to be the smallest town in England, covering only 47 acres (19 hectares). There are, however, towns with a smaller population. It also claims to have been visited by William Shakespeare, as a 'Manningtree Ox' is mentioned in Henry IV Part I.

A notorious citizen of the town was Matthew Hopkins, who gained a reputation as England's Witchfinder General between 1644 and 1647, during the English Civil War. Without much authority Hopkins and a man call Stearne travelled through East Anglia denouncing women as witches. Once accused, the women found it very hard to defend themselves, as 'justice' and 'evidence' weighed very heavily against them. The two men presided over the prosecution of some three hundred women who went to the gallows. During this short period they were responsible for more judicial deaths for witchcraft than there had been in the preceding hundred years. Every time they visited a town they were paid around twenty pounds, at the time quite a fortune and a good enough reason to find witches among a few innocent women.

The unusual three-way bridge system here on the railway is to enable freight trains from either the north or the south to gain access to the railway line to Harwich, parallel to the southern shore of the estuary. When first built, each of the three junctions was controlled by a separate signal box.

There is an extension to this walk that takes you to Flatford Mill; made famous by John Constable's painting 'The Hay Wain'.

THE BASICS

Distance: 5 miles / 8km

Gradient: Several easy slopes

Severity: Easy

Approx. time to walk: 2½ hours

Stiles: None, gates only

Maps: OS Landranger 168 (Colchester); Explorer 184 (Colchester)

Path description: Embankments, grassy fields, field edges, a short section of road and roadside paths

Start point: The car park on Riverside East, Manningtree (at the Co-op Store) (GR TM 104319)

Parking: Car park near the Co-op supermarket signposted off the High Street (CO11 1US)

Dog friendly: Good for dogs but will need to be on a lead to cross the busy A137

Public toilets: None

Nearest food: Restaurants, cafés, takeaways and pubs in the town

STOUR ESTUARY WALK

1. Climb up to the top of the embankment at the back of the car park and turn left with the estuary to the right. As the main track appears to turn left, keep ahead on a slightly lower path, between two sets of steps. Carry on under the railway and up to the busy A137.

2. Cross this busy road with care and take the path past the signpost and litter bin. Carry on with the river to the right. The path eventually comes to a junction at a metal kissing gate next to a National Trust sign and a long, low concrete structure to the right. Keep straight on with the hedge and the trees to the left to the wide hedge gap on the left.

3. Turn left across the wide concrete bridge and take the path ahead (there should be a track in the grass) to the metal gate in the hedge ahead. Go through, cross the footbridge and bear left through the gates/footbridge at the far left. Turn left, through the wide gap and right, upslope between trees, passing right of the house to the road.

4. Take the road left, under the railway. Continue upslope round a sharp right-hand bend to the signpost on the left. Turn left through this wide wooden gate, along the gravel drive between trees with the hedge to the left for 400 yards to the wooden kissing gate on the right. Go through and bear left, through the next wooden gate to the signpost this side of the road, near to the church.

5. Turn right and immediate left at the signpost next to the brick cottage, go through a wide gateway and carry on with the churchyard wall to the left, to the marker post on the right. Follow the track right, down into the dip, and bear left over Wignall Brook up to the kissing gate. Bear right, upslope through a metal kissing gate; keep ahead left of the houses and walk up to the busy A137.

6. Cross this busy road very carefully and turn left on the roadside path to the signpost where the path ends, turn right, through the gap and bear right with the path along the bottom of the slope. Go right at the marker post. The track heads back uphill across the end of a tarmac path and along the backs of the houses; follow the path right and left and follow as it leads eventually to the road. Turn left, over the railway, down to the T-junction. Cross and continue up the path to the car park straight ahead.

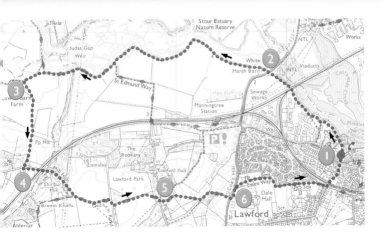

Flatford Mill Spur - see over for details of this delightful detour.

©National Trust Images Rod Edwards

The Flatford Mill Spur

It seems a pity not to include Flatford Mill in this walk, although you are venturing into Suffolk. It adds a mile to the route but adds another dimension to the walk and you can easily make a day of it by the time you have wondered around the village.

The mill, the watermill at Dedham just upstream and two local windmills were owned by the artist John Constable's father. The Dedham mill was replaced in Victorian times by the brick building now converted into flats. Flatford Mill features in several of Constable's paintings. Flatford Mill (Scene on a Navigable River), completed in 1816, shows a young boy on a horse which is towing a lighter up the river, has the mill in the middle background. The mill, nearby Willy Lott's Cottage and Bridge Cottage are all looked after by the National Trust but not open to the public. 'The Hay Wain' featuring a cart or Wain being pulled across the river, with Willy Lott's cottage to one side, was painted from the front of the mill.

Willy Lott was a friend of Constable's who never ventured far from his home, in which he had been born. He complained of poor health and had the land that he owned worked by other people and then lived frugally on the profits.

'The Hay Wain' was probably Constable's most famous painting, completed in 1821 and originally called 'Landscape: Noon'. It made no immediate impression in the British art world when exhibited at the Royal academy that year. It was exhibited at the 1824 Paris Salon and awarded a gold medal, it passed into private ownership before being acquired by the National Gallery in 1886. Normally seen in fairly small domestic print size, the painting presents quite an impact when seen life size at over six feet wide and four feet high, (185 x 130 cm).

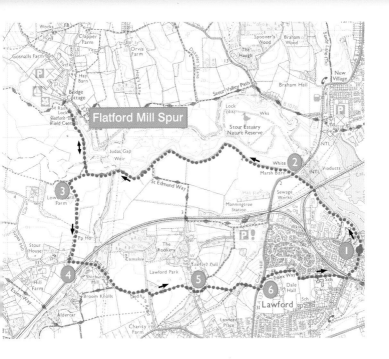

To take the Flatford Mill Spur, follow these instructions from the Stour Estuary Walk and pick up the instructions from point 3 on page 88.

1   Climb up to the top of the embankment at the back of the car park and turn left with the estuary to the right. As the main track appears to turn left, keep ahead on a slightly lower path, between two sets of steps. Carry on under the railway and up to the busy A137.

2   Cross this busy road with care and take the path past the signpost and litter bin. Carry on with the river to the right to the junction the other side of a metal kissing gate next to a National Trust sign and a long low concrete structure to the right.

    To take the Flatford Mill spur, when you get to this point on the Stour Estuary Walk you should follow these instructions.

    *At the junction on the other side of the kissing gate at the National Trust sign, bear right along the path, keeping the low concrete structure close by to the right. The path leads to Flatford Mill, half a mile away and locations of some of the most well-known British paintings.

    On your return you simply turn right and pick up the walk instructions from where you left off on the original walk.

THAXTED

STEP BACK IN TIME — THAXTED IS A TOWN WITH A SENSE OF THE MIDDLE AGES. IT HAS AN IMPRESSIVE CHURCH AT THE TOP OF A HILL, A 15TH-CENTURY GUILDHALL, A FASCINATING RANGE OF MEDIEVAL BUILDINGS AND A WORKING WINDMILL.

Thaxted is listed in the Domesday Book of 1086 as Tachesteda, which translates from Saxon/Old English as 'a place to find thatching materials'. The town is one of the few places in this country where the size of the population in the early years of the 21st century is the same as it was in Victorian times.

The church of St John the Baptist, St Mary and St Laurence is mainly late medieval, but was not fully completed until the beginning of the 16th century. Its distinctive flying-buttressed spire dominates the town. It is one of the largest churches in Essex and some locals claim that it should be the county's cathedral.

The windmill, built in 1804 on land owned by John Webb, worked for only just over a hundred years. It was put up for auction in 1907 but did not find a buyer, so gradually descended into dereliction. Restoration began in the 1970s and over a hundred thousand pounds has now been spent on the building. The sails were refitted in 1991, and a set of stones began work again in 1996. The mill is open in the summer on weekend and bank holiday afternoons.

Gustav Holst, the composer of the popular piece of classical music the Planets suite, lived in the house on Town Street marked by a blue plaque. He had been born Gustavus von Holst in Cheltenham; his grandfather was of German descent and he had been very keen to join up and fight in the First World War, but was refused on the grounds that he was unfit for service. He did, however, drop the 'von' from his name, as did most people with German-sounding names.

He befriended the local vicar, Conrad Noel, who had something of a reputation as a socialist firebrand, becoming a pillar of the church, where he sometimes played the organ and acted as choirmaster. The Holsts left Thaxted in 1925; he died in London on 25 May 1934 at the early age of 59 of heart failure, after a complicated operation on a stomach ulcer.

The Planets suite, his most popular composition, was written between 1914 and 1916. The Earth is not included as the music reflects his interest in astrology rather than astronomy. It was not performed until 29 September 1918 in the closing weeks of the war. Holst did not believe it to be his best work, and complained bitterly that the suite's popularity eclipsed all his other work.

The early history of the Guildhall is not clear; tree ring dating technology puts the date of construction at around 1460–70, refuting earlier theories that the building was mid-14th century. Thaxted was a centre for the manufacture of cutlery during the early middle ages, and there was speculation for a long time that the building was the guildhall for the cutlers. This seems unlikely as the design is technically wrong, and it is believed now that it may have simply been built as a meeting place. The hall fell into disrepair until the end of the 17th century, when it was restored by a local charity and used as a school until 1878. The building is now used for civic meetings and various exhibitions throughout the year.

THE BASICS

Distance: 3¾ miles / 6km

Gradient: Several easy slopes

Severity: Easy

Approx. time to walk: 1¾ hours

Stiles: None, gates only

Maps: OS Landranger 167 (Chelmsford); Explorer 195 (Braintree and Saffron Walden)

Path description: Grassy fields, hard paths, field edges and wider hardcore farm roads. One section goes along the grass verge of a reasonably busy road

Start point: Margaret Street car park in the town (GR TL 611312)

Parking: Car park as above (CM6 2QN). For bus services check timetables

Dog friendly: Good for dogs, but will need to be on a lead on the road section

Public toilets: In car park

Nearest food: Pubs, restaurants, cafés and takeaways close

THAXTED WALK

1. Go back to the car park entrance and turn right, take Bell Lane to the left and turn right, up Watling Street, passing right of the church. At the top at the junction with Newbiggen Street, keep straight on along the narrower section of Watling Street, bearing right, between houses. Continue straight on between hedges, out into the countryside, over the concrete bridge, passing left of the house to the marker post on the right.

2. Go through the hedge gap and turn right, along the field edge with the tall hedge to the right, bearing left to the road. Turn right, back across the stream and left down the driveway to Goddard's Farm. At the marker post take the path left, with the stream and the trees to the left, to a marker post on the left. Keep right/straight on across the field which may be under cultivation although a path should be well marked within any crop, to the junction of several farm roads.

3. Keep straight on/right up the slight slope on the wide stony farm track and bear right with the hedge now left into the corner. Bear left through trees to a driveway and keep ahead right of the houses. Continue to the road and turn right along the grass verge to the signpost on the left.

4. Turn left, past the metal barrier for 45 yards and turn left over the footbridge carry on along the right-hand field edge to the corner and take the field edge of this narrow field down to the bottom. Cross the footbridge and turn right along the field edge with the trees to the right, bearing left through the right-hand corner. Keep on this field edge with the tall hedge to the left to a marker post. Descend the steps to the left and cross both footbridges. Go back up the other side and turn right along the field edge with the hedge to the right. Exit at the far left corner of the grassy area.

5. Turn right down to the metal half barriers on the left (there is no signpost or marker post here) and turn left upslope between walls, passing left of the school

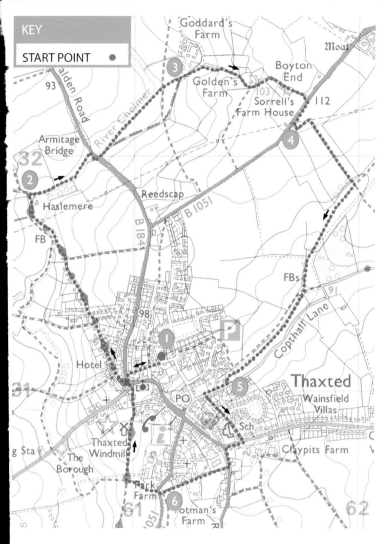

KEY

START POINT ●

and down to the road. Turn right to the B184 and cross to the roadside path, then turn left towards Dunmow, to the footpath signpost on the right. Turn right, along this hedged path down to the B1051.

6. Turn right and immediate left, past the footpath signpost, upslope towards Park Farm and The Stables. Follow the track right, to the junction and left to the top of the rise. Take the field edge right, along the track with the hedge to the right, passing right of the windmill and left of the church all the way to Watling Street, traversed earlier. Turn right, then left along Bell Lane; turn right at the end, back to the car park and the starting point.

ABOUT THE AUTHOR

I was late on my feet apparently. I didn't walk until I was 16 months old and then only when I held on to a fold in the front of my dungarees (I have a photograph!). I still have a terrible sense of balance. I have since made up for this and over the last fifteen years have walked an estimated five thousand miles. I left school at 16 and never really found what I wanted to do for a living. Apart from a short period in my early 20s digging trenches with a JCB, I spent a long time trying to sell things; car spares, garage equipment, biscuits, custard powder, spanners, deodorant, antifreeze, oil, finance, socket sets, vacuum cleaners, insurance, audio systems, washing machines, extended guarantees, televisions, books and removals.

In 1999 I was made redundant and quickly found out that no-one wanted to employ someone over 50. My wife and I already enjoyed walking; I am one of life's natural moaners and told her what I thought of some of the walking guides on offer. She very soon told me that if I thought I could do it any better I should get on with it.

The first three guides were finished just in time for the Foot and Mouth crisis and the ban on countryside activities. I eventually took the books to Peterborough and Oundle tourist information centres and tentatively asked if they were interested. They were; I had immediate orders for nearly two hundred copies of the books and have not stopped printing them since. There are now 83 books in the 'Walking Close to' series, spanning locations from East Anglia to Cumbria, Devon to Lincolnshire and Hampshire to the Midlands. The latest, two books covering the New Forest in Hampshire were published in the Spring of 2014. Total sales of the series are now in excess of 100,000 copies.